Arkwright's Cotton Mills by Night by Joseph Wright of Derby

the
Derwent Valley Mills
and their
Communities

Published by The Derwent Valley Mills Partnership, 2001.

Contents

1   INTRODUCTION   3
    1(a)   The bid for World Heritage Status   4
    1(b)   The Nomination Document   4
    1(c)   The Derwent Valley Mills and
           their Communities   5

2   JUSTIFICATION FOR INSCRIPTION AS
    A WORLD HERITAGE SITE   6
    2(a)   Significance of the Derwent Valley Mills   7
    2(b)   Comparative Analysis:
           National / International   9
    2(c)   Authenticity   12
    2(d)   Criteria under which Inscription is Proposed   13

3   THE DERWENT VALLEY MILLS AND
    THEIR COMMUNITIES   15
    3(a)   Description of Property   16
    3(b)   History and Development   72

4   BIBLIOGRAPHY   97
    4(a)   Select Bibliography   98
    4(b)   Glossary of Terms   105
    4(c)   Illustration Acknowledgements   107

Picture Left: Milford and Makeney

1 Introduction

1 (a) The Bid for World Heritage Status

In the early summer, 2000, the Derwent Valley Mills Partnership dispatched to the UK Government, for onward carriage to Paris, a portfolio of material to be laid before the World Heritage Committee of the International Council on Monuments and Sites (ICOMOS) and ultimately the United Nations Educational Scientific and Cultural Organisation (UNESCO), making the case for the inscription of the Derwent Valley Mills as a World Heritage Site. Subsequently the nominated site was visited by an international assessor, Eusebi Casanelles, President of The International Committee for the Conservation of the Industrial Heritage (TICCIH) and in December 2001 his report and the decision reached by ICOMOS will be considered by UNESCO at a meeting in Helsinki. Only then will it be known whether the Derwent Valley between Masson Mill in the North and the Derby Silk Mill in the South has achieved World Heritage status.

A successful application for World Heritage inscription would place the Derwent Valley alongside 690 sites world-wide a total which includes sites selected for natural as well as historical and cultural reasons. Of this number, there are currently 17 within the UK with a further 4 (including the Derwent Valley) currently under consideration. Two of the existing UK sites, Ironbridge and Blaenavon, owe their inscription to their industrial past while three of the current applicants, New Lanark, Saltaire and the Derwent Valley Mills share such a background. This reflects the United Kingdom Government's decision in 1997 to support a request from the UNESCO World Heritage Committee to widen the range of sites particularly in the area of industrial archaeology and the publication by the Department for Culture, Media and Sport in June 1999 of a Tentative List of sites for future nomination which included recommendations for nine industrial sites.

1 (b) The nomination document

The basis of the United Kingdom Government's case for the nomination of the Derwent Valley Mills site was contained in the nomination document, *Nomination of the Derwent Valley Mills for inscription on the World Heritage List*, which was prepared for the Derwent Valley Mills Partnership by a team of local experts drawn from the Partnership's member organisations. It included plans which defined the site and the buffer zone boundaries, planning information and management proposals but the largest single element focused

Eusebi Casanelles (centre), President of TICCIH, with Sir George Kenyon President of the Arkwright Society and members of the Derwent Valley Mills Partnership, at Cromford Mill, during his visit to assess the nominated site

exclusively on the historical importance of the site, the story of its origin and development and on a specially prepared inventory of historic buildings. In its completed form this section of the nomination document included hundreds of photographs commissioned for the World Heritage application, new research particularly for Milford and Darley Abbey and the most comprehensive account of the valley's industrial history to have been assembled. The nomination document had a limited circulation. It was not available for sale but the Derwent Valley Mills Partnership recognised that the richness and scope of the historical information it contained justified a wider distribution. Now, thanks to the generosity of two sponsors, the University of Derby and The Derbyshire and with the agreement of all those organisations which sponsored the nomination whose names are recorded inside the cover of this volume, the historical content of the nomination document has been brought together as a separate entity and published for retail sale.

1 (c) The Derwent Valley Mills and Their Communities

The new publication contains the historical sections and the bibliography and glossary of the nomination document. New pagination has been adopted and the opportunity has been taken to correct a number of typographical and factual errors and to incorporate some of the new research which has been undertaken recently into the history of the Darley Abbey Mills and housing.

The net proceeds from the sale of this book will fund future publications about the Derwent Valley mills and related topics.

The nomination process created widespread public interest and support throughout the proposed world heritage site and it is the partnership's hope that this dialogue will continue. A newsletter is published and distributed within and around the site from time to time. This contains news of the latest developments and proposals for the future. Anyone who would like to have their name added to the mailing list should contact The Derwent Valley Mills Partnership co-ordinator at the University of Derby, Cromford Mill, Mill Lane, Cromford, Derbyshire, DE4 3RQ.

Some members of the research group who assisted in the production of this volume at the Derbyshire Record Office

2 Justification for Inscription as a World Heritage Site

2 (a) The Significance of the Derwent Valley Mills

The Arkwright system substituted capital for labour, machines for skill, factory for home, and mill discipline for family work routines.

David Jeremy 1981

The eighteenth century witnessed a fundamental restructuring of economic organisation within society, resulting in the major landmark in human history that came to be known as the 'Industrial Revolution'. Amongst its many innovations was the successful harnessing of relatively large amounts of natural energy to deliver the mechanical power needed to drive machines housed in mills producing goods of superior quality at an unprecedented rate. The first stages in the establishment of this new system, the factory system, occurred at the southern end of the Derwent Valley, in Derby. Lombe's Silk Mill, when it opened in 1721, brought to England technology developed in Italy which enabled silk to be thrown on machines driven by water power. This important step towards full-scale factory production did not on its own trigger rapid or widespread economic investment in mechanised production, but its influence on the later developments in the cotton industry which took place a few miles to the north, at Cromford, is now widely recognised.

Cromford, the pre-Arkwright landscape.

The Derby Silk Mill from a water colour of 1776

It was Richard Arkwright's Cromford Mill which provided the true blueprint for factory production. Arkwright's system was copied widely in many parts of Britain and, soon after, in other countries.

The structures which housed the new industry and its workforce and the landscape created around them remain. Overall, the degree to which early mill sites in the nominated area have survived is remarkable. The value of Cromford in the nominated World Heritage Site is further enhanced by

the survival of the settlement that was constructed contemporaneously with the industrial buildings to accommodate the mill workers. Cromford was relatively remote and sparsely populated, and Arkwright could only obtain the young people he required for his labour force if he provided houses for their parents. In Cromford, there emerged a new kind of industrial community which was copied and developed in the other Derwent Valley settlements.

Arkwright's activities stimulated a surge of industrial growth in the Derwent Valley. His close association with the entrepreneurs Jedediah Strutt, Thomas Evans, and Peter Nightingale set in train a series of important developments between Cromford and Derby. All were successful industrialists, whose economic interests extended well beyond cotton manufacturing. They were also enlightened employers who displayed a strong sense of responsibility for their workforce, their dependants and for the communities that came into being to serve the new industrial system. As such, the developments at Belper, beginning in 1776-77, at Milford in 1781 and Darley Abbey from 1782, provided early models for the creation of industrial communities.

Today, the housing and infrastructure in these settlements, which were brought into being by the same economic and industrial pressures and constraints as Cromford, offer unique opportunities for comparison and analysis. In each case, there has been a high degree of survival and the number of houses of an early date, the range of the house types and the extent of the community infrastructure, are the components of an archive of bricks and mortar of unparalleled importance. Nowhere outside the Derwent Valley does the physical evidence of the early factory community survive in such abundance.

Early cotton mills were so profitable, entrepreneurs were prepared to risk prosecution for infringing Arkwright's patents to obtain a share of the market. By the time the patents were finally set aside in 1785, a 'gold rush' was in progress. This continued until boom turned to bust but by 1788 over 200 Arkwright type mills had been established in Great Britain.

Sir Richard Arkwright from a painting by Joseph Wright of Derby

The new technology crosses the sea

The dissemination of Arkwright's factory system overseas was achieved partly by the migration of skilled workmen and sometimes by piracy. Samuel Slater, 1768-1835, who had served his apprenticeship with the Strutts in Milford, and who migrated to the United States, is the prime example.

In Europe, industrial piracy played a more significant part. In Germany, Johann Gottfried Brugelmann was the pioneer. His access to the Arkwright technology was achieved through a third party who persuaded a number of Arkwright's work people from Cromford and Nottingham to move to Ratingen.

As early as 1788, according to Dr S D Chapman there were four Arkwright type mills in France and five in Germany.

The nineteenth century

The manufacture of cotton thread continued to prosper in the Derwent Valley through the nineteenth century at a level that was sufficient to maintain the mills and their communities. Some extensions to the mills were built especially after the formation of the English Sewing Cotton Company in 1897 as, for example, at Masson Mill and at Belper in the construction of the East Mill. The survival of the mills depended upon specialisation and the manufacture of sewing thread for industrial and domestic purposes rather than spinning became the main function.

As the heart of the textile industry moved to Lancashire and Cheshire, the Derwent Valley became a relative backwater. This was particularly the case at Cromford, where a combination of topographical constraints and inaccessibility limited the possibility for growth. Had the Derwent Valley rather than Manchester become Cottonopolis, there would have been a serious risk of these earlier settlements being over-run and their monuments lost, overwhelmed in the name of economic development.

As it was, though Derby itself remained a market and mill town until the second half of the 19th century when the railway industry led to a second phase of industrial expansion, further industrial growth and escalating urbanisation did not engulf the valley north of Derby. The original late 18th and early 19th century mills and the community infrastructure have survived. The cultural landscape created by the factory system remains substantially intact.

The Derwent Valley has received international recognition already. In 1994 TICCIH acted as a specialist committee on the Global Study of sites being undertaken by the World Heritage Office at ICOMOS. A list of the 24 industrial sites and landscapes considered to be of greatest international significance (and not then inscribed on the World Heritage List), was forwarded to the World Heritage Committee via ICOMOS. This included the Derwent Valley Mills.

2b   Comparative analysis: national and international

"We all looked up to him and imitated his mode of building"

Sir Robert Peel 1816

Within Great Britain the new factory system spread rapidly, and wherever it took root it was the complete Arkwright package the investors purchased. Each of the components developed in the Derwent Valley, the machinery and power transmission, the buildings, the production systems and labour management, were adopted without scrutiny. As a consequence, making comparison between the Derwent Valley settlements and other sites elsewhere is to compare siblings with the parent that gave them their being. New Lanark, a site of outstanding importance, is just such a case. It owes its existence to a visit Richard Arkwright and David Dale made to the Falls of Clyde in 1784. So impressed was Richard Arkwright with the site, he is alleged to have said "Lanark would probably become the Manchester of Scotland". The partnership with David Dale which followed, though short-lived, led to the construction of four large mills at least two of which were equipped with the Arkwright system. The similarity between the first two New Lanark mills with their projecting stair bays and Palladian windows and the earlier Masson Mill is striking.

Dale's factory settlement on the other hand owed less to its Derwent Valley forerunners and this is partly the result of a difference in the composition of the labour force Dale employed and partly the influence of a Scottish housing tradition. Unlike Arkwright, Dale employed pauper children who, by 1799, numbered nearly 500. Many of them were housed in a mill building which also served as a warehouse and workshop before specialised buildings were built to free the mill for production. Dale also built a number of tenement blocks to house the families among his workforce. Clearly the multi-storey tenement block has its origins in Scottish social and architectural tradition and does not derive from the Derwent Valley model.

The heroic phase of New Lanark's development, in the hands of Robert Owen, 1771-1858, the pioneer of enlightened mill management and factory reform, did not begin until 1799, when a partnership led by Owen acquired the mill. It was he who added the 'New Institution' for the gainful education of young and old.

New Lanark is now seen universally as a monument to Robert Owen's enlightened and radical experiments in education, factory management and social control. It is a fitting memorial and one which is not diminished by the recollection that the mill structures which survive and provide the settlement's raison d'être, derive from Arkwright's visit to the Falls of Clyde and from his own experiments in the Derwent Valley.

Stanley Mill on the River Tay, near Perth, had a similar inception. Here Arkwright's principal partner was George Dempster. Again, the partnership was short-lived, Arkwright apparently withdrawing soon after training the nucleus of

> A few days since, between 40 and 50 North Britons with Bagpipes and other music playing, arrived at Cromford, near Matlock Bath from Perth, in Scotland; .....they appeared highly pleased with the Reception they met with and had a Dance in the Evening to congratulate each other on the Performance of so long a journey.

Training was part of the service Arkwright offered his partners. In 1785 trainees from Stanley near Perth came to learn the business, as reported in the Derby Mercury.

the Stanley mill workforce at Cromford. Nonetheless, the mill which was erected at Stanley was a typical first generation Arkwright mill with an accompanying factory village. The Bell Mill, unusually for Scotland of brick above a stone base, was complete by 1790 but it was not until c.1840 that the present configuration of the site began to take shape. In its final form the complex extended around three sides of an irregular courtyard, and in its newly restored state it is among the largest of the preserved mill sites in the United Kingdom. New Lanark has, and the Stanley Mill complex will have in the future, provision for public access and facilities for education and historical interpretation.

In England, the outstanding early cotton mill site outside the Derwent Valley is the Greg's Mill at Styal. Once again the extent to which it is derived from the Cromford model is readily apparent. It was built in 1784 to house Arkwright water frames initially on a small scale. The first structure measured 8.5 m x 27.5 m and was extended in 1796. The water power was upgraded in 1801 with the result that by

1805 the capacity of what had begun as a small rural mill had grown to 3,452 spindles. Like David Dale, Samuel Greg relied heavily on pauper labour and his apprentice house accommodated as many as 100 children. In due course housing was provided some distance from the mill which by 1820 included a school and a chapel. As in the Derwent Valley communities, rent for the housing was deducted from mill wages.

Eighty years later, many of the elements of mass production pioneered in the Derwent Valley Mills were to be combined to great effect at Saltaire in Yorkshire, the most complete model village to be built for the textile industry in Britain. It expresses the culmination of the process, first started in the Derwent Valley and later developed further at New Lanark, of providing housing and social facilities for workers, which was planned from the outset and dignified by an overall architectural style. The mill was opened by Titus Salt in 1853 and was the epitome of architectural advance. It has survived better than any of its peers. Saltaire captured the imagination of all who were associated with its construction. William Fairbairn, who was responsible for much of the engineering in the mill, wrote

> *"more than 3000 persons are employed in these works, and immediately surrounding this palace of industry is a new town containing double that number of inhabitants, with all the conveniences of churches, chapels, schools, mechanics institute, baths and wash house, all of which have been established by the same spirited proprietor".*

The Mayor of Bradford, who spoke at the opening of Saltaire Mill in 1853, also had palaces on his mind. For him, the Salts had built "palaces of industry almost equal to the palaces of the Caesars!".

The international perspective

The international perspective, no less than the national context, reveals a relationship between the Arkwright system as it had developed in the Derwent Valley and the systems planted in Europe and North America which is entirely derivative. Following the Act of 1774 which prohibited the export of the 'tools or utensils' of the cotton and linen industries, the legal barrier against the export of machinery was absolute. Only by subterfuge could the transfer of technology take place. Despite the legal barriers in the summer of 1784, Johann Gottfried

Johann Gottfried Brügelmann

Cromford Mill, Ratingen

Brügelmann's mill at Ratingen (near Dusseldorf) began production and, as soon as he had secured the protection of a 12 year monopoly, he named his mill settlement Cromford. This was no defiant gesture. There were good commercial reasons behind the adoption of a name which more than any other would secure a market for his products. Brugelmann's acquisition of the Arkwright system was the work of a close friend, Carl Albrecht Delius, a German who had spent many years in England.

Cromford Ratingen's claim to be the first Arkwright mill in continental Europe remains unchallenged though there were Arkwright frames in use in France 12 months later. These were in Louviers and soon after at Valencay and elsewhere. In France, as in Germany, a number of English expatriates were at work, notably the Milne family of Stockport and two men known variously as Theakston and Flint, and Wood and Hill who had learned their business working for the Peels in Bury, though they also claimed to have been managers in Cromford. There were two particular difficulties for the French in adopting the Arkwright system. Firstly, they underestimated the management and production skills believing, until they learnt by experience, that if they secured the machines they had unlocked the secret of the system. They also lacked the skills to build the machinery, and there was a shortage of good quality castings for the gearing and moving parts, with the result in one case that workmen had to be brought in from England to complete the work.

In Czechoslovakia, the Bohemian linen and woollen trade was highly developed and extended across Europe. The cotton industry, though less extensive, was, as in other countries, the first to adopt mechanised production. It is claimed that factory spinning reached Bohemia as early as 1780, but more substantial evidence exists for the investments made by Johann Josef Leitenburger in 1796 who employed Rigo, a Danish engineer from Copenhagen, to build English spinning machines though it is not entirely clear that it was Arkwright machinery being installed.

In North America, the need for Arkwright technology was acute. By 1790, Britain possessed 2.41 million machine spindles, and the United States had less than 2000 jenny spindles and no water frames but it was not until skilled migrants, notably Samuel Slater and Thomas Marshall, both from the Derwent Valley, offered their services that the Arkwright system began to take root. Samuel Slater was one of the few who succeeded. It was his achievement to be the first in America to achieve profitability with Arkwright technology.

In the dissemination of the Arkwright factory system, nationally and internationally, a characteristic pattern emerges. The machinery and the management systems were adopted slavishly with little or no alteration. Within Great Britain, the building forms are recognisable as units within the same design system - some larger some smaller - but all part of the Arkwright family. The picture of uniformity which emerges is the product of two elements - the customer's desire to invest in a system that is known to work and the key role played by a small cadre of experts who understood the new technology. These were men like Thomas Lowe of Nottingham, Arkwright's millwright and engineer and overseers or managers from the early mills who sold their expertise to would-be factory masters.

In the export of the system abroad, the local building tradition often replaced the Derwent Valley pattern as in the New England mills, or the result could be an amalgam of Arkwright form and local style as occurred in Cromford Ratingen.

The factory housing which accompanied these mill developments did not follow a common form. This could be said to be similar to the Derwent Valley settlements which are themselves comprised of a variety of house types and

Slater's Mill, Pawtucket

have no standardised layout. There is, however, one element of the Derwent Valley's housing stock, the Cluster house, which was exported. It evolved in Darley Abbey and Belper but it is in Belper that the term 'Cluster' is first used. The Cluster house has been identified in Cité Ouvrière at Mulhouse, in Bolsterbaum in the Ruhrgebiet, and in Spain.

Fire-proofing

The fire-proof structures in the Derwent Valley, now principally represented at Belper in the North Mill, and at several of the mill buildings at Darley Abbey, are important elements in the development of fire-proofing techniques. The typology started in Derby from 1792-93, and in the West Mill, Belper from 1793-95, and was taken to a higher degree of development in 1804 in the North Mill, Belper. The oldest surviving fire-proof mill using cast iron structural members

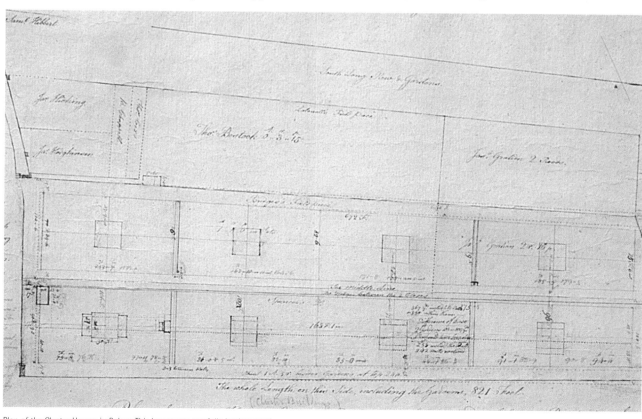

Plan of the Cluster Houses in Belper. This layout was not fully implemented.

Belper North Mill

is the Ditherington Flax Mill at Shrewsbury designed by Charles Bage, which was built in 1796-97. Bage improved Strutt's earlier system incorporating the use of cast iron beams and went on to build a further mill in Leeds, before William Strutt turned his attention to the North Mill. Bage's work in Leeds and Boulton and Watt's in Salford have not survived and Belper North Mill stands as the second oldest structure of its kind. The cast iron elements of the Darley Abbey Mills are undated at present and await further detailed investigation. They are of particular interest. In view of the close association William Strutt had with the Evans' family, there is the possibility that this was also his work.

Comparison with existing World Heritage sites

Among the industrial sites on the World Heritage List only Crespi d'Adda, in Italy, which was inscribed in 1995, shares a common history with the Derwent Valley nominated site in that it is a product of the cotton industry. It is however a late 19th century development adjacent to a cotton mill which was built in 1878. It is an outstanding example of a 19th century company town, part of the tradition which could be said to claim amongst its antecedents Saltaire and the Derwent Valley factory settlements.

2 (c) Authenticity

The nominated site meets the test of authenticity in design, materials, workmanship, setting and the distinctive character of its industrial landscape components.

The area comprises features that have been recognised by the United Kingdom government and local authorities as being of national and local cultural heritage value. The inclusion of 838 buildings on the Statutory List maintained by the

Secretary of State for Culture Media and Sport as being of "Special Architectural or Historic Interest" of which 16 are Grade I, 42 Grade II* and 780 Grade II, and 9 monuments on the Schedule of Ancient Monuments, also maintained by the Secretary of State, confirms the nominated site's status and substantially unaltered form.

The area that is being nominated for inscription comprises important mill complexes, industrial housing and the social infrastructure constructed by John Lombe in the early eighteenth century and Sir Richard Arkwright, Richard Arkwright junior, Jedediah and William Strutt, Peter Nightingale and Thomas Evans during the latter half of the eighteenth century and early part of the nineteenth century. The engineering structures through which the river Derwent and its tributaries provided power for the mills still exist, and the natural landscape setting of the industrial settlements remains largely intact, especially those components that lie to the north of the city of Derby. The Cromford Canal and the mid-nineteenth century railway, which were important in maintaining and continuing the industrial development of the mills, still retain many of their original features.

Landscape created by the Strutts at Belper

The mills and housing continue in occupation. They have by their nature, therefore, developed and will continue to develop under the influence of socio-economic pressures. The need to maintain the integrity of design, material, workmanship and setting appropriate to their outstanding universal value has been recognised in the conservation policies which are in place. No attempt has been made to reconstruct buildings that have been lost or completely demolished. Where restoration work has taken place on surviving features such as the mills, housing and farms, it has been carried out with reference to complete and detailed documentation and drawings where available, or modelled on contemporary built architectural examples.

The Derwent Valley Mills and industrial settlements are the key elements in a unique cultural landscape of outstanding universal value. The buildings and their setting are the products of the earliest attempts to develop a new industrial and social order in the factory system, and in the provision of an economically and socially viable infrastructure.

2 (d) Criteria under which inscription is nominated

The Operational Guidelines for the Implementation of the World Heritage Convention (para. 24) state that "a site which is nominated for inclusion in the World Heritage List will be considered to be of outstanding universal value for the purpose of the Convention when the Committee finds it meets one or more of six criteria". It is considered that the Derwent Valley Mills satisfies three of the criteria, as follows:

Criterion (ii) The site should exhibit an important interchange of human values, over a span of time or within a cultural area of the world, on developments in architecture or technology, monumental arts, town planning or landscape design.

The nominated site relates to developments in technology in the eighteenth century that introduced the mechanically powered factory system within the textile industry. It began with the construction of the Silk Mill in Derby in 1721 for the brothers John and Thomas Lombe, which housed machinery for throwing silk, based on an Italian design. The scale, output and numbers of workers employed were without precedent. However, it was not until Richard Arkwright constructed a water-powered cotton spinning mill at Cromford in 1771, and a second larger mill in 1776-77 using power from a tributary of the river Derwent to operate his machinery, that the 'Arkwright System' was truly established. Arkwright's mills were so efficient and profitable that they were replicated hundreds of times before the end of the century and the textile mill became the archetypal factory of the Industrial Revolution. Factory production came to dominate the manufacturing economy, not only of Britain, but also of much of the world for most of the next two centuries.

Criterion (iii) The site should bear a unique, or at least exceptional, testimony to a cultural tradition or civilisation, which is living or which has disappeared.

A view of Masson Mill by George Robertson prepared for use by Derby China Manufactory to decorate one of its products. The image in this context demonstrates contemporary fascination in the new technology and its picturesque setting.

The advent of the factory system, which developed in the textile mills of the Derwent Valley, but which spread rapidly to other locations and to other industries, created a new cultural tradition. It was one in which people, often unskilled or semi-skilled, worked on a regular shift system in large buildings and lived in nearby dependent communities. These mill villages, many of which evolved into factory towns, grew rapidly in number during the nineteenth century. From Britain, these developments moved across continental Europe and North America and spread to much of the rest of the world.

The factory, as it grew in the hands of the Derwent Valley mill owners at Cromford, Belper, Milford and Darley Abbey, brought with it a degree of social enlightenment which included a concern for the quality of life of their workforce and their workers' families and led to the provision of decent housing and other amenities.

Mill workers houses, The Hill, Cromford

Mill workers houses, Long Row, Belper

Belper and Cromford, farms and estate buildings. The settlements' special architectural and historic interest have been formally acknowledged through their designation as conservation areas.

The overall result is an ensemble of buildings, structures and settlements, all grouped within a distinctive landscape that is dominated by the river that attracted the initial investment in the area. The integrity of the scene remains evocative of the period in the late eighteenth and early nineteenth centuries when, in this hitherto obscure Derbyshire valley, the factory system was born.

Criterion (iv) The site should be an outstanding example of a type of building or architectural or technological ensemble or landscape, which illustrates a significant stage in human history.

A large proportion of the textile mills of the Derwent Valley, including some of the earliest examples known to have been built in the world, are still standing. Apart from the buildings themselves, important elements of the supporting infrastructure have survived, including the engineering structures which carried the water power systems from the river Derwent and its tributaries, and the transport infrastructure including toll roads, tramways and canals. The listing of Cromford Mill and North Mill, Belper, as Grade I, together with the inclusion of five industrial sites in the Schedule of Ancient Monuments, is recognition that they are already formally acknowledged as being of national importance. Furthermore, the factory settlements that were constructed at Cromford, Belper, Milford and Darley Abbey are almost completely preserved including in Cromford and Milford, the factory masters' own residencies and, notably in

Strutts' housing to the south east of the mills at Belper

3 The Derwent Valley Mills and their Communities

3a Description of Property

The Derwent Valley World Heritage Site nomination contains within its 24 kilometres (north to south) four industrial settlements. It extends from the edge of Matlock Bath and Cromford in the north and almost to the centre of the city of Derby in the south. The industrial settlements which are included are Cromford, Belper, Milford and Darley Abbey. The spine linking the settlements which contain the principal industrial monuments within the site is the river. Historically it was the water power which the Derwent and its tributaries offered that provided the raison d'être for the growth of these settlements.

Much of the Valley's landscape setting, valued in the eighteenth century for its picturesque quality, has survived and it forms an attractive context for the mills and their associated housing.

The Valley's late 18th century and early 19th century industrial housing has survived even more comprehensively than the mill structures. Almost as soon as they were built the Derwent Valley factory villages were seen as exemplars demonstrating the key components of community development. It was on these foundations that others in the United Kingdom and elsewhere were later to build the planned communities which have played such a large part in shaping urban industrialised society.

The 'Description of the Property' is structured in a geographical framework, travelling from north to south, following the river Derwent. The inventory begins with Masson Mill, which lies in the northern outskirts of Cromford, in the parish of Matlock Bath, and also marks the northern gateway into the nominated World Heritage Site. It continues with Cromford, Lea Bridge, Belper, Milford, Darley Abbey and finally Derby. Industrial housing, social infrastructure and farmsteads are also described within the context of each settlement. So, too, is the historic transport infrastructure of the relevant area; this includes the Cromford Canal between Cromford and Ambergate, the line of the historic turnpike road (A6 trunk road) and the railways linking Matlock-Ambergate and Ambergate-Derby (formerly The Manchester, Matlock, Buxton and Midlands Junction Railway and the North Midland Railway).

Cromford and Matlock Bath

The historic settlement of Cromford comprises Arkwright's mill complex to the east of the A6 trunk road and his industrial village to the west. Richard Arkwright's own two houses, Rock House and Willersley Castle, are located near the mill complex. The separate Masson Mill is situated

beside the river Derwent in the narrow limestone gorge between Cromford and Matlock Bath. The mills at Cromford are located in a dramatic tree-clad gorge where the Bonsall Brook cuts through the hard limestone rock to join the river Derwent.

Cromford's landscape setting

Belper's landscape setting

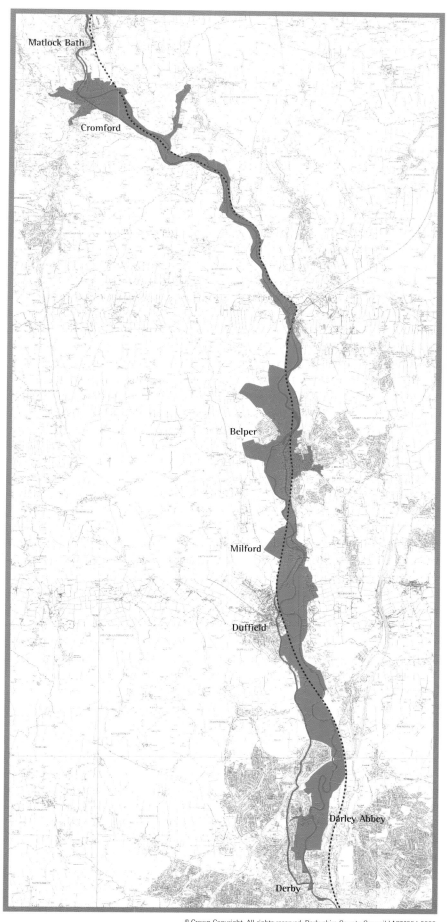

Masson Mill

1783

*Listed Grade II**

Masson Mill proclaims Arkwright's growing wealth and self confidence. Unlike the mills at Cromford, it is built on a major river, the river Derwent, which offered Arkwright the opportunity of a power source ten times greater than he enjoyed at his Cromford site. Externally, its design reflects a deliberate movement towards conscious architectural style, and its overall layout, incorporating the staircase and ancillary services in a central projection leaving production floors uncluttered, was an important advance on the early 'Cromford' style mills. Constructed in brick on a gritstone base, with stone quoins and window dressings, the original 21 bay 5 storey building was 43.8 metres long and 8.4 metres wide.

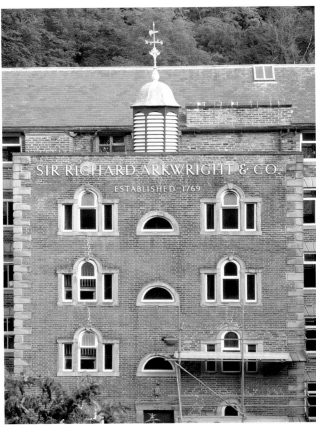

Masson Mill

The central 3 bays are advanced and have been given a decorative architectural treatment with a small lunette window between Venetian windows on each floor. It is capped with a cupola beneath which hung the mill bell. The mill was powered by a single waterwheel which, by 1801, had been replaced by two, a system which continued (with replacement wheels by Wren and Bennet in 1847) until turbines were installed in 1928. In its original form, the mill was built with a high parapet which concealed a low pitch roof but probably at the same time as the second wheel was added c. 1800, the roof was raised, as a result of which the mill acquired a useable sixth storey.

Buildings were added to the north and west of the mill by c.1835, some of which were subsequently demolished. In 1911, 1928, and more recently in 1998, extensions were added in Accrington brick. The mill chimney dates from 1900, and this and the engine house were the work of Stott and Sons, the famous mill architects. The mill has been extensively repaired and restored recently. The mill is now home to a museum and a retail village.

"So now, where Derwent guides his dusky floods
Through vaulted mountains, and a night of woods,
The Nymph, Gossypia, treads the velvet sod,
And warms with rosy smiles the wat'ry God;
His ponderous oars to slender spindles turns,
And pours o'er massy wheels his foamy urns;
With playful charms her hoary lover wins,
And wields his trident - while the Monarch spins.
First with nice eye emerging Naiads cull
From leathery pods the vegetable wool;
With wiry teeth revolving cards release
The tangled knots, and smooth the ravell'd fleece;
Next moves the iron-hand with fingers fine;
Combs the wide card, and forms the eternal line;
Slow with soft lips, the whirling Can acquires
The tender skeins and wraps in rising spires;
With quicken'd pace successive rollers move,
And these retain, and those extend, the rove;
Then fly the spoles, the rapid axles glow;-
And slowly circumvolves the labouring wheel below'

Erasmus Darwin, 1731-1802, scientific genius, doctor and poet, knew Richard Arkwright as a friend and in 1785 was instrumental in bringing Matthew Boulton and James Watt to support him by giving evidence in his two patent trials. The Botanic Garden was widely acclaimed, establishing its author as leading poet of the day. In 1797 Coleridge described him as "the first literary character in Europe and the most orginal man".

Masson Weir

Listed Grade II*

Masson Mill has an outstanding landscape setting in the wooded valley of the river Derwent, enhanced by a weir which is unusual on account of its convex shape. It is thought to have been built in this form because of the underlying rock structure at this point in the river. It is likely to have been an early addition to the Masson site, if not contemporary with the mill itself. The earlier paper mill on part of this site would not have justified the construction of a weir on this scale.

Unlike the mills at Cromford, the building of Masson Mill did not lead Arkwright to construct workers' housing nearby. Most of those who worked in the mill lived either in Cromford in houses owned by the Arkwrights or in settlements nearby such as Matlock Bath or Bonsall.

There is some evidence that cottage accommodation was created near the mill to take advantage of the economic opportunity created by its success. In 1784, Thomas Pearson began building a cluster of cottages close by. His son-in-law made later additions. A short row of formerly back-to-back houses at South End survives from this development.

The Cromford Mill Complex

Cromford Mill was the world's first successful water-powered cotton spinning mill.

The Cromford Mill Complex was built on an elongated site, constricted by cliffs to the north and south. It comprises a series of linked mills, and warehouses and workshops built between 1771 and 1790. Severe perimeter gritstone buildings enclose and define the mill yard, their height and the paucity of ground floor windows providing tangible evidence of a concern for the security of the works. The area as a whole presents an unusually complete picture of an early textile factory complex.

The First Steps

Richard Arkwright and his partners leased a small site in Cromford close to an existing corn mill in August 1771. It was served by the Bonsall Brook and by the water from the Cromford Sough, a lead mine drainage channel, neither of which produced a large volume of water but which had the advantage of offering a constant supply with minimal seasonal variation.

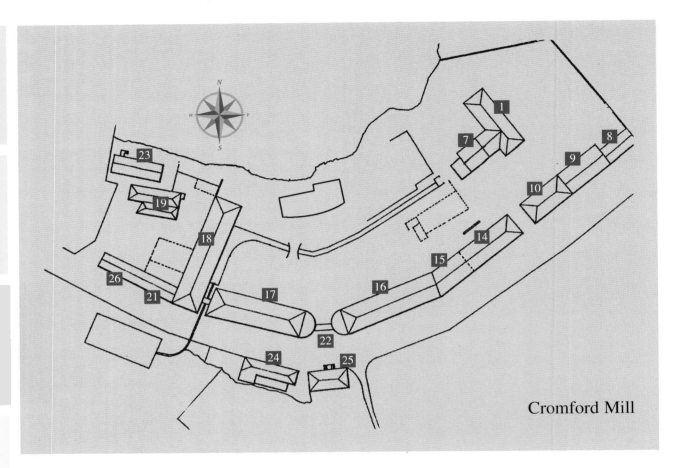

Cromford Mill

The first buildings on the Cromford Mill site were the upper mill, a weaver's workshop (demolished when the first mill was extended) and some cottages, the remnants of which survive in building 24 (see plan).

The Upper Mill

1771
Listed Grade I

The upper mill, in its original form, contained 11 bays with external dimensions of 28.5 metres x 7.9 metres; it was five storeys in height. It was built of coursed gritstone and was lined with a skin of brickwork. It was entirely traditional in its construction, with timber beams and roof members and sash windows. A water-colour representation of the mill indicates that it bore a cupola for the mill bell on the roof at the southern end. In the late 1780s the mill was extended by 4 bays and an additional power source added. It is a simple functional structure with few concessions to architectural style save for the original main entrance - what Richard Arkwright called the "First door" - which has a fine Gibbsian doorway, and the mill windows which have slightly arched wedge lintels with voussoirs; the central bays project forward slightly on the elevation which faces towards Cromford.

The Upper Mill from a water colour by William Day C.1789

The Upper Mill awaiting repair

Gibbsian doorway to Upper Mill

Upper Mill from the mill yard

Upper Mill from the west

Upper Mill before the fire of 1929

The Lower Mill from a water colour by Zachariah Boreman 1787

The Annexe to the Lower Mill

A fire in 1929 removed the two upper storeys of the building after which it was re-roofed in asbestos sheet and returned to use manufacturing colour pigments. Recent research suggests that the mill was, from the beginning, powered by an overshot wheel with water brought to it by aqueduct. Such an aqueduct would have passed narrowly above Richard Arkwright's "First door", quite spoiling the effect of the fine masonry; but given the choice, it is entirely characteristic of the man at this stage of his career that the power source was considered more important than the architecture.

The Lower Mill and Annexe

1776 and c.1790
Listed Grade I

Richard Arkwright used the five years between the construction of his first Cromford Mill and the planning of the second to develop his mechanised cotton spinning processes, and the size and scale of the second mill bears witness to his need for additional space and additional power - and to his confidence in his new systems. The new mill, 36 metres long and 8 metres wide, comprised 16 bays and was 6 storeys high with an additional clerestorey attic. The lower courses were of stone, but it is not clear whether the upper section was built in brick or in stone.

Recent excavation has revealed the ground plan of the mill including the wheelpit, offices and two privies. Further research will ascertain whether the pit contained one or two wheels and whether the gable end, which remains to be investigated, included a heating system.

The second mill annexe, stone-built in 4 storeys, contains an unusually complete hot-air heating system. It was constructed within the staircase turret and adjacent to the lavatory block. Whereas in the second mill, the staircase and offices were placed within the main rectangle of the mill plan, thus reducing production space, the second mill annexe - by using a central service tower - left each mill floor unencumbered.

Mill/Warehouse Building 17

1785-90
Listed Grade I

This large stone building of 5 storeys is believed to have functioned as a mill with powered machinery on the four upper floors. On the ground floor, there was a storage area at the end of the building nearest the gate associated with receiving and opening bales of cotton. The cotton was cleaned in a sealed working area inside the large doors towards the middle of the building. A space with an underdrawn ceiling, doorway to the road and enlarged windows would seem to have been an office or possibly the dinner house.

The apsidal end of the building contained the staircase which served the upper floors. Here again is a design solution which offered maximum production space within the mill. At the other end of the building, adjacent to the watercourse, an internally constructed lavatory column served each floor. Beside it is a hot-air heating system similar to that which survives in the second mill annexe. The building was linked to the first mill above first floor level by a bridge built in brick. Only the lower section of this bridge has survived.

Building 16

1785-90
Listed Grade I

The apsidal end which is the most prominent feature of this three storey stone-built structure housed a staircase serving the first and second floors and, through the second doorway in the apsidal end, provided entry to what is likely to have been the mill counting-house. The large windows are indicative of this function, as is the surviving fireplace and evidence of panelling. It is likely that the building was originally divided by a large arched opening in the ground floor and that the area to the east of the door would have been used for warehousing, as would the floors above.

The Bridge

Listed Grade I

A brick arched bridge links two floors of building 17 to the upper two floors of building 16. It spans the entrance to the site providing additional security above the gates. A Guardian insurance plaque is mounted on the roadside face of the arch.

Building 15

c.1800
Listed Grade I

This three-storeyed stone building with sash windows links buildings 14 and 16. It is clearly later than either of its neighbours. It contains significant remains of a hot-air heating system which may have served both this building and the adjoining building 14.

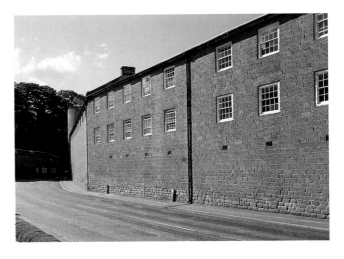

Building 14

c.1790
Listed Grade I

This three-storeyed stone building is thought to have accommodated workshop space on the ground floor. The upper floors show signs of having been used for machinery, possibly knitting frames. The building was originally linked at first and second floor level by a bridge to the second mill.

Building 10

c. 1790
Listed Grade I

Archaeological evidence suggests that this three-storeyed stone building was constructed and used as a warehouse. The second floor windows remained unglazed until the 1980s, protected solely by internal shutters. Once its textile function had ceased, it is known to have been used to store cheese awaiting shipment on the canal, and later timber.

Buildings 8 and 9 (The Restaurant)

c. 1790
Listed Grade I

The original use of this building was as a stable and coach-house. It has now been incorporated into the Cromford Mill restaurant.

Building 24

Listed Grade I

Within the shell of this building the remains have been found of a three-storey cottage which is assumed to have been one of the cottages built by Richard Arkwright in 1771. Subsequently the building became the coach-house and stables for the manager's house after which Cromford Colour Co. converted it to a laboratory. It now houses office accommodation.

Building 25 (Mill Manager's House)

1796
Listed Grade I

Beyond the aqueduct stands an urbane, three-storey, 3-bay building. Its perron, iron railings and lamp holder, together with the nearby limestone sett paving and cannon-pattern cast iron stoop, gives texture, interest and counterpoint to the plain cliff-like walls of the mill. Overlooking the entrance to the mill yard it provided added security to the site.

Aqueduct

1821
Listed Grade I

The aqueduct in its present form, with a cast iron trough resting on stone piers, replaced an earlier structure which is known to have had a timber launder. The aqueduct carried water from the Cromford Sough to power the first mill. There is archaeological evidence to suggest the existence of a structure running at a lower level than either the present cast iron or the previous timber aqueduct.

The Barracks

c.1786

The 'bow-fronted' building was in existence by 1786. It was badly damaged by fire in 1961. Subsequently it was demolished, but not before it had been photographed by the Royal Commission on the Historical Monuments of England (RCHME). Oral tradition has it that this was the barracks: the accommodation for the unmarried male workers of the mill who lived too far from home to travel from work each day.

The foundations of this structure have been excavated and consolidated as part of the conservation and interpretation of the Cromford Mill site.

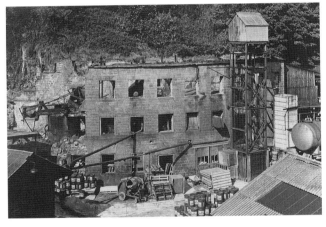

The Bridge, Cromford Mill Yard

Early 18th century
Listed Grade I

The bridge pre-dates Arkwright's development of the Cromford Mill site. It bridges the Bonsall Brook, and originally carried the public road which linked Matlock Bath to Cromford Bridge and to the road to Wirksworth. When Arkwright constructed his second mill in 1776-77, the new building blocked the road. It was soon after this development that he improved the alternative route between the Cromford road and Matlock Bath by cutting through a

section of Scarthin Rock, so creating a more manageable route for wheeled vehicles. The road through Scarthin Rock was not cut down to valley level until 1818, when the turnpike road to Belper was constructed.

Building 23 (Loom Shop)

1776-86
Listed Grade I

This three-storey stone building stands to the west of the first mill. The generous provision of two-light mullioned windows suggests it was a loom shop. Richard Arkwright is known to have employed weavers to work up his yarn and it is likely that this building replaced an earlier structure which stood between it and the first mill, and which is known to have been built as part of the first phase in 1771.

Building 19 (Two brick cottages)

c.1780
Listed Grade I

A prestigious brick-built double-pile structure which stands in front of the loom shop and the first mill. It is likely to have been used to provide residential accommodation for those whose work at the mill required a constant presence, such as gate-keepers or watchmen. In its original form, before the addition of the second pile, it matched the building on the roadside known as Grace Cottage; together they offered the appearance of matching 'pavilions', flanking the mill and enhancing its appearance when seen from Cromford Market Place. Joseph Wright's representations of the mill by night and by day indicate how much of the mill would have been visible from higher up the valley before the engineering works associated with the creation of the turnpike road, now the A6, destroyed the natural slope of the valley from Cromford Market Place to the Mills.

Building 26 (Grace Cottage)

c.1780
Listed Grade I

A brick cottage similar to its neighbour but rendered, and with the original hipped roof concealed within a modern structure. It is the Arkwright Society's intention to restore Grace Cottage to its original appearance in due course.

The Mill Basin Weir and Culverts

Listed Grade I

Much of the investment in the Cromford complex was associated with the engineering structures which delivered and carried away the water which provided the motive power for the mill machinery.

The basin weir c.1777, in the middle of the mill yard, the wheel pits of the first mill extension c.1786 and second mill 1777, the culvert which took water to the Cromford Canal c.1820; in particular, the massive culvert 1777 which runs from the second mill into Cromford Meadows and on to the river Derwent though for the most part unseen, are all features of outstanding historical importance.

Richard Arkwright's Factory Village

Arkwright's industrial settlement at Cromford

Arkwright established his industrial settlement in Cromford over a period of 20 years. The first significant house-building was in 1776 in North Street, followed soon after by the three-storey houses towards the top of Cromford Hill. From 1776 until 1789 Cromford was owned by Peter Nightingale, and it was not until Sir Richard had purchased the estate that the pace of development accelerated. Nor is it possible until that time to discern any element of conscious planning in the community's development. The village continued to grow under the stewardship of Richard Arkwright junior, and by the time of his death in 1843 it had acquired the size and shape it was to retain until well after the Second World War. It is fortunate that most of the modern housing development in Cromford has taken place in areas which are largely separate from the historic community.

The Market Place

c.1790

The Market Place provided the heart of Arkwright's community. It extended right across the road and pavements and included the area to the East. The main bulk of the development within this part of Cromford dates from c.1790. The market which Arkwright started in 1790 was an integral part of his strategy for the development of Cromford and was fundamental to the success of his pioneering achievements. In order to attract the families which were to provide his workforce, it was not enough to supply good housing. It was also necessary to ensure that there was a regular supply of provisions, and this was achieved by attracting traders to the Cromford Market and building the new commercial premises which would retain them.

The Greyhound Hotel, Market Place

1778
Listed Grade II*

Unambiguously the principal building of the Market Place development, a dignified pedimented, three-storey building, constructed in sandstone with a Roman Doric doorcase and raised quoins.

The Greyhound provided lodging for visitors to Cromford and was used as the location for festivities organised by Sir Richard for his workforce. The Arkwrights also used it for business. It was here in the public room that Richard Arkwright junior instructed Georgiana Duchess of Devonshire to leave her answer as to how she intended to repay the money she owed him.

The Arkwright Stores, 39 The Market Place

1780s
Listed Grade II

One of a row of six houses, converted for retail use in the 19th century. Constructed in coursed gritstone with slate roofs. The two bowed shop windows are a rare survival from the early 19th century. Originally it had a slate roof.

The Market Place, nos. 28-36

c.1790
Listed Grade II

Three-storey gritstone houses built as part of Sir Richard Arkwright's Market Place development with later inserted shop-fronts. Originally they had slate roofs.

The Market Place, nos. 20-26

c.1790
Listed Grade II

A rare example of a single-storey range of Georgian shambles. The range is constructed of regular coursed gritstone with a hipped slate roof. A similar structure once stood in the other corner of the Market Place where the Cromford Community Centre now stands.

Willersley Castle, Willersley Lane,

c.1790
Listed Grade II*

William Thomas. Interior Thomas Gardner of Uttoxeter.

A mansion house located on rising ground and set in a Grade II landscaped park. It was commissioned by Sir Richard Arkwright, who died before it was completed. It is constructed of ashlar sandstone. The central facade is defined by projecting turrets. Contemporary observers described Willersley as "an effort of inconvenient ill taste" and "a great cotton mill". The Arkwright family occupied the castle until after the First World War. In the grounds of the castle the stable block and home farm buildings (though not the farmhouse, which predates the Castle), by Thomas Gardner of Uttoxeter, survive though in an altered form. It is now in the ownership of Christian Guild Holidays.

Lodge to Willersley Castle, Willersley Lane

c.1792
Listed Grade II

Thomas Gardner of Uttoxeter

A picturesque lodge to Willersley Castle. It has an ashlar facade; the remainder is coursed rubble.

The Fishing Lodge, Mill Road

c.1796
Listed Grade II

A small gritstone structure standing by the ruins of the 15th century bridge chapel and created from an earlier range of farm buildings. The fishing lodge was fashioned by Richard Arkwright junior to function as a dwelling for his water bailiff. By the early nineteenth century it was in use as a workman's cottage. It is a copy of the fishing lodge on the River Dove made famous by Isaac Walton and Charles Cotton. The inscription over the door lintel reads "piscatoribus sacrum" - sacred to fishermen.

Rock House, Mill Road

1776
Listed Grade II

Built by Peter Nightingale for Richard Arkwright, it became his home during his time in Cromford. It was extended in the 19th century. A three-storey brick and ashlar house constructed on a cliff, it overlooks the Cromford Mills in stark contrast to Willersley Castle which, though constructed in an elevated location, is entirely hidden from the mills and almost entirely from the village. It has been converted to flats.

North Street

1776
Listed Grade II*

The first of Sir Richard Arkwright's workers' housing in Cromford. The street consists of two long gritstone terraces which face each other across a broad street, comprising 27 dwellings in all. The accommodation is superior to rural housing in Derbyshire at this date and North Street set a pattern for what was to follow elsewhere in Cromford, though it exhibits a higher standard of construction and design than some of the later houses in the community. The mixture of leaded lights and sashes on two storeys and doorways which echo classical design features, convey a social pretension which would not have been lost on the skilled workers Arkwright sought to attract to Cromford. Sash windows would have been generally reserved for farmers or the commercial classes in this part of Derbyshire at this time. Provision for domestic accommodation was on

the ground and first floors with workshop space on the top floor, characterised externally by distinctive 'weavers' windows'. These workshops enabled members of the family not employed within the mills to earn an income. When these houses were built they were intended for weavers and their families.

Weaver's windows, part blocked up   104 The Hill

Cromford Hill 104, The Hill

c. 1780
Listed Grade II

A three-storey terraced house constructed in coursed gritstone with a tiled roof. This is one of 83 similar dwellings within the settlement. Unlike the earlier houses in North Street, the houses on Cromford Hill provided purely domestic accommodation with no workshop space. The terrace forms part of a long linear arrangement of different housing forms constructed by the Arkwrights on either side of Cromford Hill.

Cromford Hill 122, The Hill

c.1810
Listed Grade II

Part of the second generation of Cromford industrial housing. These two-storey terraced cottages, two cells deep, were constructed in coursed gritstone with Welsh slate roofs. This is one of 36 similar dwellings within the village.

Cromford Hill, nos. 37 and 39, Victoria Row, The Hill

1839
Listed Grade II

Pair of houses within a row of eight built for Richard Arkwright junior to accommodate workers in the textile mills. They were constructed in coursed rubble with render and have cast iron windows with opening casements. They are set back behind front gardens which divide them from Cromford's main thoroughfare, The Hill. The rear elevation has small single-light windows to the upper floors with low lean-to sculleries.

Staffordshire Row, nos. 30–46 Water Lane

Late 18th century
Listed Grade II

A row of three-storey gritstone houses similar in form to those found on The Hill. Richard Arkwright acquired the land on which these cottages stand in 1784 and is believed to have built this row to house mill workers.

Arkwright's Houses on Water Lane

Early 19th century
Unlisted

These are three-storey, semi-detached houses, stone-built and rendered. Six houses follow this pattern; all are on

Water Lane. With their substantial gardens, relatively spacious accommodation and privies, they are believed to have been provided for the overseers or foremen in the mill, Cromford's equivalent of the Darley Abbey and Belper cluster houses - though, of course, they are less innovative in design.

St Mary's Church, Mill Lane

1797 and 1858
Listed Grade B

Founded by Sir Richard Arkwright as a private chapel within the grounds of Willersley Castle and opened to public worship by his son in 1797, the church was substantially altered and partly gothicised in 1858. It has an extensive system of mural decorations by Alfred Hemming, of 1897, depicting scenes from the Bible. A memorial to Mrs Arkwright (1820) by Chantrey hangs on the north wall of the nave. In the corresponding position on the south wall is a similar plaque dedicated to Charles Arkwright (1850), by Henry Weeks. Sir Richard's remains were moved from Matlock Church to St Mary's and interred in a bricked-up vault within the chapel.

School and School House, North Street

1832 and later
Listed Grade II

The School

The school was built by Richard Arkwright junior to provide accommodation for the young mill workers who, under the terms of new legislation, were to be required to work under the 'half-time system', whereby part of each day was to be spent at school and part at work. The school was extended in 1893. Both the school and the school house are constructed of gritstone with hipped slate roofs. The School House is accommodated in one of two wings attached to the main building.

The Village Lock-up, Swift's Hollow

1790
Listed Grade II

A two-storey three-bay building constructed of coursed gritstone with a graduated Derbyshire slate roof. It was originally built as a terrace of three cottages early in the 18th century, but in 1790 the ground floor of the centre cottage was converted to a village lock-up. The lock-up contains two small cells with metal doors. One cell retains its original bunk, which is suspended from the walls by chain. The lock-up, the adjacent space and the room above have been renovated by the Arkwright Society and the upper floor is now in commercial use.

Privies to the rear of 56–76 Cromford Hill

Listed Grade II

Sandstone privies built in pairs and roofed with monumental gritstone slabs.

Pigcotes, Swift's Hollow

Late 18th to early 19th century
Listed Grade II

Sandstone pigcotes constructed as part of the Arkwright community development. Pigcotes played an important part in the cottage economy of a village such as this. They are situated amongst allotments, small barns and workshops.

The 'Bear Pit'

1785
Listed Grade II

The Bear Pit, as it is known among Cromford residents, was constructed in 1785 by Richard Arkwright. It consists of a more or less oval stone-lined pit sunk into the course of Cromford Sough, a lead mine drainage channel, across which a dam and sluice have been erected. The dam forced the sough water back into a new underground channel which connected the sough to the Greyhound pond. By this means Richard Arkwright was able to supplement the water stored in the pond with sough water. He used the device each Sunday while the mills were not at work so that the Greyhound Pond was adequately supplied when work began again on the Monday morning.

The Greyhound Pond

c. 1785

The principal supply of water for the cotton mills was from Cromford Sough. The first mill was powered exclusively from that source until, from the mid 1780s, it was extended and a second wheel added. This wheel derived its water from the Bonsall Brook via an underground culvert

controlled by a sluice in the corner of the Greyhound Pond (adjacent to the present day Boat Inn). It is not easy to date the construction of the Greyhound Pond. It may have been one of the ponds referred to by William Bray in 1783, but he may have had in mind the ponds created on the Bonsall Brook for the corn mill which had been erected in 1780. Certainly, the Greyhound Pond must have been in existence by 1785, when Richard Arkwright incurred the wrath of the lead miners by damming the Cromford Sough at the Bear Pit so that he could force the sough water into the Greyhound Pond. The culvert Arkwright built for this purpose can be seen from Water Lane to the rear of the Greyhound coach-house and stable-block.

Former Corn Mill, Water Lane

1780
Listed Grade II

This water-powered corn mill with its attached cottage was built by George Evans in 1780. It is constructed in coursed rubble and squared block gritstone with ashlar dressings; the living accommodation had Venetian windows of which one has survived intact. The kiln adjacent to the corn mill was in existence by 1797. The maltings, now the Cromford Venture Centre, was added in the 19th century. It is interesting to note that the corn mill was constructed within two years of the destruction of the Cromford corn mill to make way for the second cotton mill.

Slinter Cottage, Via Gellia

c.1800
Listed Grade II

The mill was originally constructed as a lead slag mill associated with a lead smelting enterprise higher up the valley. It was later converted to wood turning and produced bobbins and pulleys for the cotton mills. It is set in an area of great natural beauty dominated by Slinter Tor. The adjacent woodland has been designated an SSSI and an SAC. The structure still retains a small breast-shot wheel with wooden buckets. The cottage is in the course of renovation by the Arkwright Society.

Cromford Station buildings and footbridge

c.1855, 1860, 1874 and 1885
Listed Grade II

In 1849 the Manchester, Matlock, Buxton and Midlands Junction Railway opened a line to Rowsley passing through Cromford. The station-master's house and the up line waiting room were built in c.1855 and 1860 in coursed gritstone with slate roofs. The design by G H Stokes bears witness to his work in France with his father-in-law Joseph Paxton in the 1850s.

The station buildings on the down line were built in 1874 and are now leased as a Venture Scouts Activity Centre. The Butterley Company erected the ornate footbridge in 1885.

Cromford Bridge Hall (formerly House), Lea Road

17th century with later additions
Listed Grade II

Once known as Senior Field House, it is a 17th century hall and crosswing house with dormer gables - perhaps containing the remains of an earlier building. It is built of

coursed gritstone. Some 17th century mullioned windows with transoms survive. In the 18th century wings were added at both ends. The addition at the east end was built in a similar design to the adjacent 17th century crosswing so as to give the overall impression of a symmetrical main front.

The main entrance was placed in the middle of this enlarged facade. Most of the windows are sashed and it has a recently repaired stone slate roof. Most of the building is three storeys high. The house was acquired by George Evans, brother and business partner of Thomas Evans, founder of the Darley Abbey cotton spinning mill, in c.1760. It was lived in by his descendants including his daughter Elizabeth Evans, a local amateur artist and great-aunt of the famous Florence Nightingale.

Woodend, Lea Road

1796
Unlisted

Built by Peter Nightingale, founder of the Lea Cotton Mill as a replacement for Lea Hall, which he found too cold in the winter months. The house, which is three bays in width and three storeys in height, is built of ashlar gritstone with corner and front door quoins. It has sashed windows with stepped lintels. There are 19th century additions; also a separate coach-house with stabling, which has undergone recent alterations. After Nightingale's death it was occupied for a time in the 19th century by the Smedley family who took over Lea Mills.

The Cromford Canal

The Cromford Canal ran 23.3 kilometres from Cromford to the Erewash Canal at Langley Mill. The 10.5 kilometres of canal between Cromford and Ambergate which lie within the nominated World Heritage Site was constructed in the early 1790s under the direction of William Jessop assisted by Benjamin Outram. The canal was intended as part of a through route to Manchester but it was not until the Cromford and High Peak Railway was constructed between 1824 and 1830 that this vision became a reality. The Cromford Canal promoters sought to unlock Derbyshire's

immense mineral wealth, especially its limestone. Apart from the obvious advantages to Sir Richard Arkwright for his mills, he too saw the opportunity presented by exporting lime and sought a monopoly in this trade on the canal in return for which he was prepared to lend his name to the promoters of the canal project. Only when he was finally persuaded that such a monopoly would be against the law did he agree to give the canal scheme his energetic attention. He also agreed to sell most of his garden to the Canal Company to construct the Cromford Wharf. With his assistance the Canal Bill was steered through Parliament in the face of considerable opposition.

The canal had a profound influence on the economic growth of central Derbyshire achieving a substantial outreach by means of its many wharves and linking tramroads. Thus Belper, apparently bypassed by the canal, derived huge economic benefits from it.

The canal terminus abuts Mill Lane opposite Cromford Mill. Cromford Wharf incorporates two warehouses, an office or counting house and two cottages. Once enclosed entirely by a stone perimeter wall, the wharf was home to a range of other facilities; these buildings have not survived.

The Cromford Canal Wharf

Canal Warehouse

1794
Listed Grade II

The warehouse was built soon after the canal opened for Nathaniel Wheatcroft, who was to become the principal canal carrier.

It is built of coursed, squared and dressed sand-stone with two storeys and half basement and is roofed in graduated Welsh slate. The elevation visible from Willersley Castle has an embattled parapet and this feature has led to the structure being known locally as 'the gothic warehouse'. It was used to receive goods brought in by the canal boats and awaiting onward transport. The lean-to shed over the canal was added in 1814. The building has been restored by the Arkwright Society.

Warehouse

c.1824
Listed Grade II

A two-storey, three-bay, warehouse in coursed dressed sandstone, with a slate-hung cantilevered projection overhanging the feeder arm of the canal. It was built soon after the feeder arm was added. It was used to store goods awaiting transport by boat which, thanks to the overhanging section of the building, could be loaded under cover. The warehouse was equipped with a crane, now replaced by a modern replica. The building has been out of use for many years and is awaiting restoration by the Arkwright Society.

The Counting House

Part c.1794: part late 19th century
Listed Grade II

A two-storey polygonal structure in coursed dressed sandstone with a Welsh slate roof. Its unusual shape is explained by its proximity to the culvert which once brought water to the canal from the Cromford Mill basin and by the limited space between this and the canal wharf gates, of which the two massive stone posts have survived.

The building was restored by the Arkwright Society, which uses it as an office.

Cromford Canal Wharf Cottages

1796
Listed Grade II

Two canal cottages built for the Cromford Canal Company soon after the canal opened and later extended to accommodate company administrative staff. One of the cottages has been carefully restored and has regained its original appearance.

The Cromford Canal: features south of Cromford Wharf

Accommodation Bridge

c.1792
Unlisted

South of Cromford Wharf the coursed stone accommodation bridge with a string course and parapet, believed to have been built c.1792. There are others of similar design along the line of the canal. A notable feature of this bridge is the evidence in the stonework of wear caused by the canal boat tow ropes.

High Peak Junction

The Cromford and High Peak Railway which opened in 1830, completed the link to the Manchester area the canal promoters had intended to provide. It crossed the high ground between Cromford and Whaley Bridge by means of a series of inclines and stationary steam engines. These were linked by level sections on which the wagons were hauled by horses. The junction was created to provide a link for trans-shipping goods between the Cromford and High Peak Railway and the canal. A later link connected the junction to the railway between Ambergate and Matlock.

On the west side of the canal there are several buildings which served the needs of the railway and most notably the railway workshops. This group of buildings was built, re-built and enlarged between c.1830 and c.1865. In the first instance the workshop served the needs of the inclined plane railway and horse-drawn wagons. Later when steam locomotives were introduced to the line the workshop's functions were extended. The buildings are of coursed gritstone and brick. Inside the building there are surviving examples of the original fish-bellied cast iron rails used on the Cromford and High Peak Railway. The workshop houses a small museum which is open to the public during the summer months.

Warehouse

c.1850
Unlisted

The warehouse which stands between the canal and the railway was built c.1850 to replace an earlier canal building. It is now used as a residential study centre. It is built of coursed stone and has a covered canopy under which railway goods would have been loaded to protect them from the weather. It also has a load height gauge for the railway. Adjacent to the warehouse is a larger open shed supported by cast iron columns. Adjacent on the north side are the remains of the base of a crane.

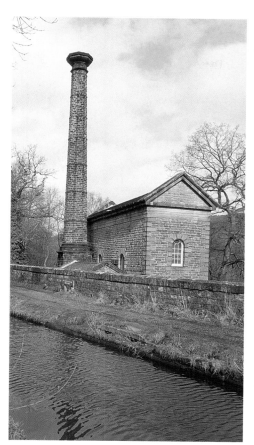

To the south is a building of c.1850 in coursed stone which was used as railway offices. Further south on the canal is a paved spillway over which surplus water was discharged from the canal into the river.

The Leawood Pumphouse

1849
Listed Grade II and a Scheduled Ancient Monument*

The Leawood pumphouse, engine and chimney, are situated south of High Peak Junction and on the east side of the canal.

These structures were built in 1849 to house a steam pumping engine to increase the supply of water available to the canal. The pedimented pumphouse building is of ashlar gritstone with chamfered quoins. It has a square-headed doorway with pilasters and quoined round-arch windows. The adjacent boiler house has arched doorways. The engine was constructed at the Milton Ironworks by Graham & Co. It is a Boulton and Watt single action beam engine which is maintained in operational condition and is put in steam from time to time.

The Pumphouse Chimney

The 29 metres high engine chimney is built of coursed stone and has a cast iron parapet.

The Wigwell Aqueduct

1793
Scheduled Ancient Monument

The Wigwell Aqueduct over the river Derwent was first constructed in the early 1790s. By September 1793 serious cracks had appeared. William Jessop, the engineer who had supervised the building work, accepted liability and offered to re-build it at his own expense. He claimed the fault lay with the Crich lime he had used as mortar which did not set. Iron cramps were used to give the structure greater stability, and following this remedial action there has been no further serious trouble. The structure is 182.9 metres long, 9.1 metres high and supported by three arches. The one which spans the river is nearly 73 metres in length. There are two date stones above this central arch.

At the southern end of the Wigwell Aqueduct the junction with the Leawood Arm of the canal may still be identified. This branch, which was built by Peter Nightingale in 1802, extended the canal to a wharf at Lea Bridge. It serviced the Nightingale leadworks and mills. When the closure of the canal was proposed in 1910 by the canal's then owners, the Midland Railway, the businesses at Lea Bridge were among the principal objectors, the canal having become an essential link for the import of coal and other raw materials. Their protest was unsuccessful and parliamentary approval was given for the canal's closure.

Lengthman's Cottage

c.1830
Listed Grade II

At the junction of the Leawood Branch with the canal is a
lengthman's cottage, now without a roof. It is proposed that
this structure should be conserved as a picturesque ruin.

The Canal Aqueduct over the Railway

c.1850
Scheduled Ancient Monument

The aqueduct which carries the canal over the railway was
constructed c.1850 when the line was built. It has a cast
iron balustrade on the south side, the upper rail of which is
a piece of railway rail.

Canal Tunnel

c.1792
Unlisted

The canal tunnel is about 73 metres in length and was
built of coursed stone. It has coursed stone ramparts
and is barrel- vaulted. A raised towpath runs through
its entire length.

The Meerbrook Sough Portal

1772
Scheduled Ancient Monument

It was the completion of the Meerbrook Sough which, being at a lower level than the
Cromford Sough, drained most of its water and so put the Cromford Mills out of business,
at least for water-powered uses. The sough tunnel was constructed over a long period
from 1772 to c.1841. The portal may well have been constructed in 1772 as the
dated keystone suggests. It bears the legend "FH1772" which refers to Francis
Hurt who was the sough proprietor at that time.

Lea Bridge

Smedley's (formerly Nightingale's) Mill

1783
Unlisted

The 18th century cotton mill at Lea Bridge is so concealed by
later buildings that it is visible now only from the air. Yet
within the interstices of the Smedley factory the original
mill has survived surprisingly intact. It was planned and
built in 1783 by Peter Nightingale, Richard
Arkwright's financier and landlord in Cromford;
and Benjamin Pearson junior, hitherto one of
Richard Arkwright's trusted employees. It
was not an enterprise that Arkwright

Lea Mills, water power
system, c.1860

Lea Mills today. The original mill is highlighted

had authorised and he pursued Nightingale through the courts; but the mill continued to operate. It was built on the Lea brook, a stream which already powered a lead smelting mill and a rolling mill both in Nightingale's possession, but which was capable of further development. During 1784 and 1785 the stream's capacity was enhanced by the creation of two dams higher up the valley, and there was a further substantial investment in 1792 with the creation of a third dam for the cotton mill. It was as a result of this development that the existing corn mill ceased to operate and Nightingale created a new one higher up the valley on a site that is now known as Pear Tree Farm.

Much physical evidence of these developments remains. The dams and watercourses are discernible on the ground and the lead smelting site is visible in the form of slag heaps even though all the buildings have gone; so also have the mills below the cotton mill, of which the hat factory was the largest. The cotton mill itself, however, has enjoyed an extraordinary longevity.

In 1818 it was taken over by the Smedley family, who after a decade attempting to make a success of the business as a woollen spinning mill adapted it for the production of cotton and wool yarns, from which the Company's knitters made high quality knitwear. This was the work of John Smedley (1803-1874) who, from successful experiments in the 1820s in mixing cotton and merino wool, was able to produce a range of high quality products. John Smedley was content to sell his knitwear through the great hosiery houses such as Brettles or Morleys, but after his death the firm gradually developed its own retail brand for which it is now known world-wide.

Of all the first generation Arkwright sites in the Derwent Valley only at Lea Bridge has there been continuous textile production. Lea Mills remains a major source of employment in the area.

Housing at Lea Bridge: Four cottages adjacent to Smedley's Mill

1783
Listed Grade II

Three cottages built to an L-shaped plan were erected in December 1783 at a cost of £110 as part of Peter Nightingale's cotton mill development. They are strikingly similar to the three-storey cottages built at the same date on the upper slope of Cromford Hill, with mullioned windows on each floor. This row is roofed in Derbyshire stone slate, as the Cromford houses may once have been. A fourth dwelling has been added at a later date with single large windows in each of its two storeys, which spoils the symmetry of the elevation. These cottages have been unoccupied for many years.

Middle Row

1791
Listed Grade II

A row of six three-storey cottages (originally a row of four, but extended at the upper end of the terrace at an early date), built by Peter Nightingale in 1791 as part of the expansion of his cotton mill enterprise. Like the earlier row which they overlook they have two-light mullioned windows. Each cottage has a massive quoined door surround and plain plank door with a single opening window above. There are some modern renewals. These cottages remain in use as dwellings.

Belper

Belper is located half way between Cromford and Derby. The river Derwent
and the A6 trunk road, a former turnpike, run along the western edge of the
town. The Strutts' mill complex and the greater part of the associated
housing is all to the north of the town centre, with the houses stretching out
in rows and terraces up the slopes of the hills to the north and the east.
Jedediah Strutt and after him, his sons, William, George Benson and Joseph,
developed the mills over a period of about 40 years between 1777 and 1815.
Thanks to William Strutt's innovatory talents as an engineer the site included
a range of structures. Taken together, they charted the evolution of mill
design from the traditional stone and timber structures through to the first
steps in fire protection and onto the full use of iron and brick-arched fire-
proofing. Few of these buildings survived the clearance of the site c.1960.

The Strutt factory communities in Belper and Milford have survived almost
without loss. The houses, the farms and public buildings, together with the
documentary material which has been collected, represent a unique archive for the industrial and social historian. The
survival of the Strutt housing has been underpinned by the quality of the buildings the Strutts commissioned. If the houses
had been built to a low specification they would have been superseded a century ago, victims of the legislation to improve
basic housing standards and of public demand for better quality housing. As it was, the Strutts retained their inheritance,
repairing and improving their housing stock from time to time until the 1950s when the family began to dispose of its
property and the houses gradually became owner occupied.

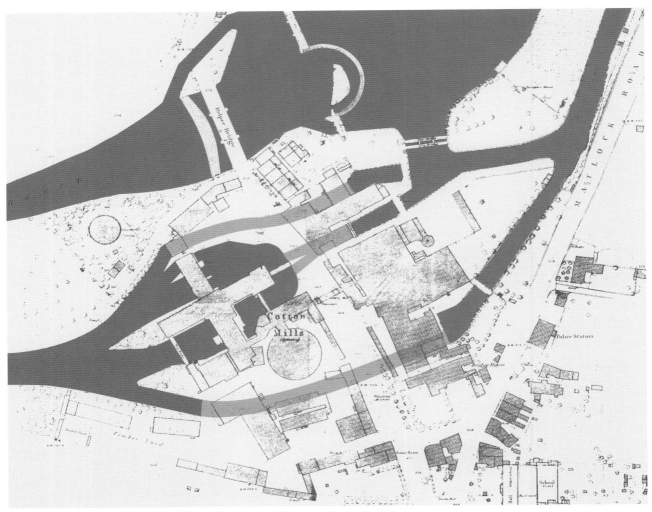

The extensive water power system of the Strutts' Belper Mills, as shown on the Ordnance Survey 1:500, 1880

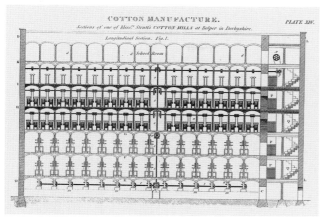

Cross section of Belper North Mill from Rees' Cyclopaedia

Belper North Mill

1804

Listed Grade I

Belper North Mill, rebuilt in 1804 by William Strutt on the lower storeys of the earlier mill that had been destroyed by fire in 1803, embodies the knowledge accumulated from all the earlier experiments William Strutt had made into fire-resistant mill structures and from his close participation in Charles Bage's pioneering work at Shrewsbury. William Strutt, 1756-1830, was a mechanic and engineer of the highest distinction. He was the first to tackle systematically the threat of fire in textile mills first by cladding with plaster and then by the use of iron and brick. His work with Charles Bage, whose family had close connections with Darley Abbey and who he may have known from an early age, was seminal in the evolution of fire-proof design.

Basement

It was Charles Bage who produced the first iron-framed mill at Shrewsbury in 1796 and then went on to build a further mill in Leeds. William Strutt's Belper Mill embodied much of what Charles Bage had learnt and took further the evolution of these structures from which there emerged, two generations later, the first fully framed building, the Sheerness Boat Store.

The mill is constructed in brick on a stone plinth. The exterior retains the character of the earlier mill and so has the appearance of a first generation Arkwright-type structure. Every aspect of the building was designed to resist combustion. It has a T-shaped plan consisting of a main range of 17 bays and a wing of 6 bays. Housed within the wing is the wheel chamber that occupies the three bays adjacent to the main range.

Cast iron column

The wheel pit, which now stands empty, gives some indication of the power once generated to operate this mill. The wheel installed in 1804 was replaced in 1823 at a cost of £1,383; it was constantly repaired as daily use took its toll. In the basement, the former ground floor of the earlier mill, stone piers carry the cast iron columns which support each of the floors above. The massive stone buttresses which were once a feature of this space have been removed.

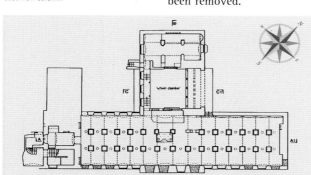

Plan of basement

The floors are composed of brick and tile supported by arches that spring from cast iron beams. The beams are supported by cast iron columns which, in turn, are linked together by wrought iron ties. Clay pots are used to infill the floor arches in the bays above the water wheel so reducing the weight in this area.

Carl Friedrick Schinkel, arguably the greatest German architect of the 19th century and a member of the Prussian Public Works Committee, visited England in 1826. Schinkel described the Strutt works in Belper as "the best in England". The sheer scale of iron-framed industrial buildings throughout the country impressed him and influenced many of his later designs, notably the Bauakademie, 1831-5 in Berlin. The mill has also attracted more recent attention. Sir Neil Cossons in 1981 described it as "the most beautiful, sophisticated and technically perfect structure of its era".

William Strutt was recognised by his contemporaries as the leading exponent of hot-air heating systems for large buildings and the stove, which was once located in the windowless masonry block occupying the two northern bays of the western end of the North Mill, is of some interest, though it is now recognised that mill buildings of an earlier generation, as for example those at Cromford, had hot-air heating systems before William Strutt's experiments began. The archaeology of the stove-housing and stoking area in the North Mill have been disturbed in modern times, which complicates the historic evaluation of this area of the structure. A stove which was part of a William Strutt heating system has survived and is now in the National Museum of Science and Industry in London.

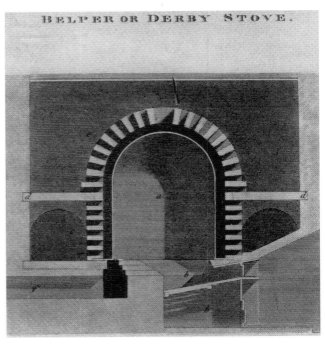

William Strutt's design for a heating system

The Belper East Mill

1912
Listed Grade II

The East Mill completely overshadows the North Mill. A fortress-like, seven-storey building with four corner turrets, Italianate tower and rows of windows, it was constructed by the English Sewing Cotton Company in 1912 in the distinctive Accrington red-brick, which had by this time become the preferred building material for textile mills - whether built in Lancashire or elsewhere. It is built around a steel frame, which by 1912 had long been entirely free-standing; unlike William Strutt's structures, which relied on the walls of the building to support them. Nevertheless, its debt to the earlier innovations of Strutt and Bage is palpable.

Arched footbridge

c.1795
Listed Grade II*

A sandstone bridge linking the two separate areas of the former Strutt Mills complex on either side of the Ashbourne Road. The archway also served a defensive role. Along its length are gun embrasures which protected the West Mill counting house.

The Horseshoe Weir

1797

Listed Grade II*

The two first mills in Belper, the South Mill and the North Mill, were served by the water retained by Jedediah Strutt's first weir, a simple structure which spanned the river near the present day railway bridge.

To power the West Mill, Strutt needed a new and very much larger weir. An outline of this structure appears on a plan of 1796, and building began soon after. As the name suggests, the weir is of distinctive shape. It was modified and increased in height in 1819 and 1843 yet remains largely unaltered. The weir and its associated watercourses altered the river significantly. By 1820, some 5.8 hectares of water had been added to the Derwent immediately above Bridge Foot. Rees's Cyclopaedia, which was published serially between 1802 and 1820, described the mills at Belper as being "on a scale and most complete we have ever seen, in their dams and their water works". It is one of the outstanding engineering structures of the late 18th century.

The Strutt industrial settlement in Belper

Modern Belper represents at least four phases of development: the original medieval rural settlement of Beaurepaire that centres on the chapel of St John; the later growth lower down the hill which, by the middle years of the 18th century included a market place on a lower level than the present one; the industrial community established by Jedediah Strutt in the late 18th century on the northern edge of the existing settlement and around Belper Bridge Foot and up Belper Lane; and the 19th century expansion of the commercial centre along King Street and Bridge Street.

The most prominent of the Strutt industrial housing stands on land to the south of the mill complex and to the east of the Derby-Matlock road. The land was acquired largely through numerous individual purchases, with its end use for workers' housing clearly in mind. The houses were all of a high standard with gardens and, in certain areas, allotments for the residents. The housing, constructed from Derbyshire gritstone or locally made brick, and roofed with Staffordshire blue clay tiles or Welsh slate, was largely placed in an east-west alignment connected by narrow passages giving an almost grid-iron character to the layout. Construction of housing by the Strutt estate continued into the 20th century.

The houses vary in form from row to row as the Strutts experimented with different designs. The result is a visually cohesive, attractive and unique mix of workers' housing.

As well as the land on the slopes to the east of the mills, the Strutts had also by the 1790s acquired land and property and started to build housing on the south facing slope to the north-west, adjoining their Bridge Hill estate. Here, by 1840, they had built or acquired up to 100 houses which were rented to their workforce. The housing in this area was developed plot by plot as land became available. Most of it was built in short terraces of three or four houses, mainly in gritstone, though some are in brick, on levels up the hillside formed by earlier quarrying or along Belper Lane and Wyver Lane. Good examples can be seen in the terraces in the Scotches: in the stepped terraces on the northern side of Belper Lane, culminating in the cluster block which housed the original Belper Parish Workhouse; and in the small groups of houses such as Pump Yard, set back from Belper Lane.

Also of interest is the brick terrace on the southern side of Belper Lane which still retains the arch which was a former entrance to Bridge Hill house. These houses have the appearance of being built for estate rather than for mill workers.

Belper Lane, nos. 54-92 (formerly Mount Pleasant)

c.1790

Listed Grade II nos. 54-56, 58-62, 64-66, 82-84, 86-92

A series of stepped terraces built in stone, some doublefronted and some single, roofed in slate. These houses have large gardens and cellars.

Mount Pleasant

Old Workhouse, nos. 94–100, Belper Lane

1803
Unlisted

Back-to-back cluster type houses, stone-built, with a central chimney and three-storey. This was the parish workhouse until replaced by the Union Workhouse, now the Babington Hospital, when it was sold and put to domestic residential use.

Pump Yard

Belper Lane, nos. 74–80

By 1818
Unlisted

North side brick stepped terrace in the ownership of the Strutts by 1818.

Pump Yard

Belper Lane, nos. 68–70

By 1818
Unlisted

South side. Stone terrace of two, in the ownership of the Strutts by 1818.

Belper Lane, nos. 25– 33

By 1818
Unlisted

Five houses in a terrace which was in the ownership of the Strutts by 1818; brick with stone slate roof, of two-storeys and with an archway over the central section, thought to be part of the carriage-way to Bridge Hill House. This feature was restored in 1818-19.

The Scotches, west side

Belper Lane, nos. 5–8

c.1819
Listed Grade II

Four three-storey stone-built houses in a terrace, with a house of two storeys at the western end. By 1844 these houses had associated nailers' workshops.

Wyver Lane, nos. 3, 5 and 7

By 1818
Listed Grade II

Three (formerly four) terraced houses which were in the ownership of the Strutts by 1818. Of three storeys and stone-built with slate roofs and brick chimneys. Each has an allotment bounded by dry stone walls on the other side of the lane.

Derwent Terrace, nos. 6, 7 and 8; also 9 and 10

By 1818
Unlisted

Stone-built in rubble and coursed stone; purchased by the Strutts sometime after 1818.

Back Wyver Lane

By 1818
Unlisted

A terrace of four two-storey houses, originally with adjacent nailshops. It was acquired by the Strutts sometime after 1818.

Wyver Lane

'Weir Lodge Houses', 39 Wyver Lane

By 1818
Unlisted

Formerly two, in a stone-built terrace of two storeys and with a large brick chimney stack. In Strutt ownership by 1818.

Short Rows, nos. 46 and 47

c.1788
Listed Grade II nos. 26-36, 38-47

One of the first groups of houses to be constructed by the Strutts in Belper adjacent to the chapel of 1788. The Short Rows originally comprised four separate rows of largely one-up, one-down cottages containing 47 houses in all. The houses are built in red-brick with slate roofs and brick chimneys.

Mill Street, nos. 18-20

c.1788
Listed Grade II nos. 2-20

Two rows originally containing 25 houses of two-storey red-brick houses, which originally formed part of the Short Rows (see above).

Former Police Station, Matlock Road

c. 1848
Listed Grade II

Located in a prominent position opposite the Strutt Mills, the Police Station was the first of its kind in Derbyshire. The building is constructed in ashlar with a slate-clad hipped roof.

Bridge Foot, nos. 18 and 20

c.1800
Listed Grade II

Built as three cottages which were later used as a cottage hospital run by the Strutt family. A long red-brick building with a slate roof.

The Chapel and Chapel Cottage, Field Row

1788
Listed Grade II*

The Chapel was built by Jedediah Strutt and, apart from the mills, is believed to have been one of the first buildings which he constructed in Belper. Sometime after his arrival in Belper Jedediah adopted the Unitarian faith. The building is a striking example of austere nonconformist architecture built in ashlar with a hipped slate roof. The Chapel was extended on each side early in the 19th century so that in its present form it is three times its original size. The facade to Field Row has a round-arched entrance with a keystone. An external cantilevered stone staircase gives access at first floor level to the gallery. A marble plaque commemorates the life of Jedediah Strutt. The catacomb below the chapel contains the remains of a number of members of the Strutt family including, it is thought, Jedediah himself.

The Chapel cottage which adjoins is thought to have been built soon after the Chapel itself, though the kitchen extension, which is housed in a vaulted space beneath the Chapel, cannot have been constructed until the Chapel was extended early in the 19th century.

Long Row   1792-97

Listed Grade II

This is industrial housing of a high quality. There were originally 77 houses in the Long Row. It was built in the form of three terraces, two of which were continuous until broken by the North Midland Railway in 1840.

The 35 three-storey houses are constructed

predominantly in sandstone with a continuous sloping eaves line. They are designed with interlocking plans formed around the staircase.

The southern two-storey terrace is constructed primarily in brick and ascends the rising ground in stepped pairs. Each house has its own garden with allotments behind.

There are 62 dwellings in all.

Joseph Street, nos. 5 and 6

The Clusters

1805
Listed Grade II

A plan of August 1805 by James Hicking indicates that it was the intention to build 32 cluster houses in eight blocks of four houses each. In the event only five blocks were built and with some significant variations from the original plan. The plan does not indicate the provision of privies or pigsties, nor is it clear that each block is to have a lean-to outshut at each end.

The houses are designed on the innovative plan first implemented in Darley Abbey of one block divided north-south and east-west to form four back to back houses. Each block is sited in the centre of a large plot and, as they were built, each house has a building in the garden incorporating a privy and a pigsty.

At 7 Joseph Street the privy and pigcote have survived in a building constructed in coursed stone.

The term 'Clusters' was in use by 1820 and the buildings may have borne this name from the outset though this is not clear from Hicking's plan on which the words have been added by a later hand.

Nailshop

Joseph Street, no. 8

Early 19th century
Listed Grade II

The nail maker's workshop, a rare survival, is constructed of coursed stone with a tile roof, brick chimney and cast iron windows. This is a single nailshop; far more typical in Belper were the rows of nailshops, perhaps five or six under a single roof, but no more than two or three of these have survived, all of them altered drastically.

As early as 1790 Strutt had built a nailshop next to one of his cottages. His interest in nailing was solely to provide work for the male members of the families inhabiting his cottages. There is also evidence he invested in framework knitting workshops to achieve the same purpose.

Crown Terrace, nos. 4–13 (formerly Smith's Court)

1794-95
Listed Grade II

A terrace of three-storey stone houses built by the Strutts for their mill workers. The houses are constructed in pairs on an interlocking pattern in a similar style to the three-storey houses in Long Row. In 1890 the Strutt estate extended the properties to the rear except the two houses nearest to the A6 road.

Field Row, no. 6

c.1788
Unlisted

Two terraces, 1-7 and 8-13 three storey red-brick houses standing adjacent to the Strutt Chapel and in marked contrast to the nearby houses in the Short Rows. On the basis of the rent paid these were among the more expensive Strutt properties.

Chevin View, nos. 1-10
(formerly Berkin's Court)

1790
Listed Grade II

The shells of 10 of these houses had been completed by March 1790. These are an early example of back-to-back housing, a building form of which the Strutts made very limited use. They are of three storeys and built of coursed sandstone with slate and blue tiled roofs. Only nos. 9 and 10 have retained their original form. At one time Chevin View contained 18 houses.

George Street, nos. 1-12

1840-42
Unlisted

These two-storey stone and brick-built houses built between 1840 and 1842 were constructed in a single terrace with a roof line and eaves which follow the slope of the ground. They were built on the ground which had previously been set aside for the cluster houses and until George Street acquired its present name in 1899 were known as New Houses, Cluster Buildings. The present stone extensions were added probably in the 1890s.

George Street, nos. 13-24

1898
Unlisted

Some of the later Strutt housing built in Belper. These two-storey brick houses with bay windows and verandas were built on the former Potato Lots (allotments).

Wyver Farm

By 1809
Listed Grade II

Situated north of the town of Belper, the farmstead was built by the Strutt Estate. The farm was in Strutt ownership by 1818, but it is not known when the present buildings were erected.

It demonstrates many of the features for which the Strutt farms are famous: the stone fire-proof construction of the ceilings and floors; the careful arrangement of feed storage for ease of delivery; and the use of natural ingredients allowing feed such as wet grains, cereals or hay to be tipped into pits or carted into stores that open into the first floor mixing room above

the cow byres. The cow byres are well ventilated - another Strutt design feature.

The main part of the farm complex comprises an L-shaped group built into the hillside and enclosing a north-west facing yard. The group is constructed of stone with slate roofs. The east and south ranges consist of cow byres with loading bay and hatches opening into the yard and rows of ventilators with iron grilles opening into the cow byres just below the first floor level. Both ranges have arched stone ceilings supporting the stone floor lofts above. Eight feed drops in the south wall serve the cow byres below. At the west end of the range, to the rear, three brick-lined wet

grain pits are dug into the slope with doors into the loft where the food was mixed. The western range comprises a stable block with a stone floor and separate feed storage areas.

An east-west range of buildings comprises a wagon lodge, stable and barn. This also is constructed of coursed stone and has a slate roof. The four-bay cart shed has been added to the main range and has a lower roof level supported on four cast iron pillars which have been inserted on massive stone bases.

Other subsidiary buildings include a small stable, free-standing cow-house, hen houses and piggeries.

To the left, Crossroads Farm; to the right, Dalley Farm

Crossroads Farm

Crossroads Farm

Post 1818
Listed Grade II* Farmhouse. Grade II Farm buildings

Crossroads Farm is located on the outskirts of Belper, to the west. It is not shown on a map of 1818 and the land was not in Strutt ownership at this date. The design and construction of the farm buildings benefited from the techniques pioneered by William Strutt using cast iron components to achieve a fire-proof structure. Externally, massive stone outbuildings flank the handsome ashlar farmhouse. The interior has evidence of ironwork within its construction, notably within the kitchen ceiling which is formed of stone slabs fitted into iron beams. The roof of the hay barn incorporates iron trusses and the farm buildings utilise cast iron columns and brick-arched floors.

Dalley Farm

Post 1819
Listed Grade II* North wing of house and farm buildings

The farmstead lies close to Crossroads and though it was constructed predominately early in the 19th century it was created from an existing 17th century building. The farm was not in Strutt ownership in 1819. The farm contains numerous features of design and construction which are characteristic of the Strutt model farms: the stone vaulted ceilings and flag floors for fire protection; the systems for moving feed stores to feed mixing; the iron roof supports and the unique range for housing wet grain.

The building complex planned around two yards with an L-shaped group to the north east is for the most part constructed of stone with slate roofs. The L-shaped group consists of a four-bay shelter shed with a flagged floor opening onto a yard. Stone pillars with cushion capitals support the roof. One central pillar supports the ridge.

The west-facing range comprises a hay house open to the west and a four-bay hay barn with an open front supported on a pierced shallow-arched iron beam with iron posts dating from 1876.

The north-south range comprises a threshing barn with a wooden threshing floor and straw barn above, a wet grain store with some brick construction and a cow byre with six feeding hatches into the feeding passage. To the north there is a three-storey block under east-west facing gables, containing mixing rooms below and a feed store above.

The ceiling is stone vaulted and the ground and first floors are flagged. Round holes in the floor with metal trap doors allow feed to be dropped through to the mixing room. One of these holes is over a stone mixing trough in the angle between the east-west range of cow-sheds dividing the yard. The roof is supported on semi-circular arches by cruciform-section iron pillars.

The later brick-built wet grain store contains nine feed bins for the storage of wet grains for cattle feed with nine stone-framed pitching holes to the east and west allowing for the delivery of grain and wide, iron-framed, openings onto a passage allowing for shovelling out.

The northern cow-house has stone gables and brick south wall and features a mixture of small original metal windows and later larger ones which cut through the rows of ventilation slits. Iron cruciform-section pillars support the roof of the hay house.

Another cow-house divides the north and south yard and abuts the ashlar carriage entry that links the house to the farm buildings. This carriage entry is of a buff-coloured stone rather than the original pink stone and is a later insertion to increase the status of the building. A further cow-house which forms the east side of the northern yard is built of brick with a walkway supported on brick and stone columns.

Transport Features in Belper

The North Midland Railway, which opened in 1840 on a route between Derby and Leeds surveyed by George and Robert Stephenson, the pioneer railway engineers, passes through the nominated World Heritage Site between Derby and Ambergate. It contains numerous engineering structures of the highest quality which were the work of the Stephensons and their supervising engineer, Frederick Swanwick.

Railway cutting walls

1840
Listed Grade II (in part)

The route of the railway through Belper was the subject of lengthy negotiation between the Strutts and the North Midland Railway company. The details are obscure, but it would appear that the company's first proposals were unacceptable to the Strutts and had to be modified. The line was to have been driven through Belper to the west of Bridge Street, crossing under Bridge Street near Crown Terrace and finally leaving Belper close to the school buildings on Long Row. Such a line would have been clearly visible from Bridge Hill House and it may have been this which forced the Stephensons to reconsider their

proposals. In the end a line was chosen which kept the railway well to the east of Bridge Street and in a cutting throughout all of its length through the town.

An agreement with the Strutts compelled the company to design each of the bridges carrying the streets severed by the line in such a way as would not alter the existing slope of the street. The result is an impressive man-made "gorge" with sides of rusticated stonework with a stone band carried round from bridges and internal buttresses. Most of the original bridges have survived.

Railway bridges

1840
Listed Grade II

Spanning the railway along the cutting are a number of fine original bridges. Road bridges span the railway at Field Lane, where the north parapet has been replaced by a metal guard, George Street, Gibfield Lane, Joseph Street, Long Row and William Street. A footbridge spans the railway at Pingle Lane. The construction of the bridges generally comprises an elliptical arch in rusticated rock-faced stone with ashlar copings, impost bands, quoins and voussoirs.

Milford

Milford to the East of the River

The Strutts started purchasing land in Milford in March 1781 and immediately began to construct the first structure in what was to become a complex of cotton mills and bleach works. At this point along its course the river had long been put to use to provide the power for industrial processes and Strutt's first acquisitions were two of these sites, the New Mills and the Makeney Forges and the Hopping Mill Meadow which included a fulling mill. Some cottages came with these properties and there would have been some local labour available but it cannot have been long before there was a demand for more accommodation to house an expanding workforce. In Milford, in addition to the houses the Strutts built, further mill workers' housing was built by local people responding to the economic opportunities the Strutts created.

On the east side of the river the land rises steeply, and the Strutts had little alternative but to construct their cottages in terraces which follow the natural contour and run parallel to the road and the river. On the west side, a less severe slope enabled the community to develop along more flexible lines although the housing here also followed the existing road pattern.

The actual layout is likely to have been determined more by the availability of building plots than by the convenience of the location or by planned development. In 1791, the Enclosure Award brought to the market much land in Milford and the Strutts were well placed to seize this opportunity.

The houses and farms which formed the Milford factory settlement have survived substantially intact with little demolition, though some of the houses have been altered unsympathetically. By contrast, the industrial sites which were for so long the economic hub of the community have been reduced by the clearance of c.1960 to a handful of later buildings and a range of archaeological features. On the former cotton mill site, two wheelpits remain, together with the base plates of William Strutt's suspension bridge of 1826 which was removed in 1946. Only the foundry the Strutts established c.1825, on Hopping Mill Meadow, has continued in use in the ownership of Hepworth Heating. To the south of the former cotton mill site, the Strutts' flour mill built on the Makeney Forge site to replace the Duke's corn mill which they had demolished, remains.

The list which follows is a selection rather than a comprehensive inventory of the places of worship, public houses, farms and cottages constructed in the late 18th and early 19th centuries. A number of buildings which have been excluded from the list are, however, identified on the Milford plan.

Foundry Lane, Derby Road, nos. 2 and 3,

c.1818 in present form
Listed Grade II

A pair of semi-detached houses constructed from, or on the site of, an earlier farm which was purchased by the Strutts in 1818. They are of coursed stone with a tiled roof with off-centre chimneys and of two storeys. The ground floor windows are of iron set in wooden frames with some opening casements, with smaller iron windows above.

Duke's Buildings

1822-23
Listed Grade II

Numbers 2 to 8 Duke's Buildings, Derby Road were built on land the Strutts purchased in 1818 from the Duke of Devonshire, hence the name. They were built between 1822 and 1823 at a cost of £466 a pair and are of three storeys in coursed stone with brick chimneys, but most of the roofs have been replaced. Number 2 forms part of an interlocking house plan with number 65 Hopping Hill (West Side). It also has a fire-proof 'pot' floor in the third storey.

Hopping Hill, (East and West) Terrace, nos. 1-26

1818-20
Listed Grade II

This back-to-back terrace was built by the Strutts between 1818 and 1820. The terrace is built into a steep hill side. The east side (nine double-fronted houses) is of two storeys. On the west side (14 houses) the houses are of three storeys. They are built of coursed stone with slate roofs and brick chimneys.

Two of the many cast iron street signs which have survived in Milford

Hopping Hill, nos. 1-4

Millford Mill Site and Hopping Hill

In an ingenious interlocking plan the cellars of every other house on each side are dug into the hill side. Some iron casements and sash windows survive. The approach to this terrace can be made by a substantial stone staircase flanked by enormous coursed stone walls and iron posts. Each house also had a garden plot divided again by substantial stone walls and steps. Some small stone-built sheds survive in the gardens: probably, originally, earth closet lavatories. At the north end of the terrace a wide stone paved embanked chute from the road enabled carts to tip their loads into the yard.

Hopping Hill (North East side), nos. 1–30 and 31–52

1792-97
Listed Grade II

This early industrial housing was built between 1792 and 1797 on land Jedediah Strutt received from the Enclosure of the common land and by purchase from Tristram Revell. There are two separate terraces of 28 and 29 houses. Both are built of coursed stone with a stepped roofline. They have slate roofs and brick chimneys. All are of three storeys, although numbers 2-7 have small gabled attic dormers. Each has one window on each floor at the front and casements at the rear. The first floor windows vary between casements and smaller sashes at the front and rear. There are casements on the second floor of the front elevation. These are said to be Strutt designed and are nine-paned iron windows, four panes of which form each casement. It is clear that though they are of an early date they are not original. The first floor windows have voussoirs. Some modern alteration has taken place to the windows. On the rear elevation evidence survives of an original exit to the garden at half-landing level by means of a bridge.

Number 28 is double-fronted and shaped to accommodate the road which ran between it and number 29 which once housed the Milford Provision Company, the Strutts' Co-operative. The manager lived on the premises and his assistant next door at number 30. On the present garage site was a warehouse, stable and slaughterhouse.

Hopping Hill (South West side), nos. 57–64 (consecutive)

Early nineteenth century
Listed Grade II

These houses were built in the early 19th century by the Strutts on land purchased in 1791. They are built in coursed stone with brick chimneys and are two storeys high, though number 57 has three storeys with the same roofline. Numbers 61 to 64 (consecutive) have dormers. A stockinger's shop survives at the rear of number 64.

Houses around the East side of the bridge

1792-1859
Listed Grade II

The cluster of buildings around the Post Office, some of which have been restored recently, were built between 1792 and 1859 by speculators building on an enclosure allotment taking advantage of the economic opportunity created by the Strutts' investment in Milford.

Housing at Makeney

Forge Cottage, Makeney Road

c.1830
Listed Grade II

It was built c.1830 on the site of an earlier building, near the site of Makeney Forge. A coursed stone house, it has modern stone eaves and a slate roof, cast iron adjustable gutter brackets and cast iron casement windows set in wooden frames. It was purchased by the Strutts in 1855.

Forge Hill, Makeney Road

1791
Unlisted

Originally a double-fronted house which was built by Samuel Crofts on an enclosure allotment. A shop was subsequently added. The building was purchased by Anthony Radford Strutt in 1819 and converted to three houses.

Forge Hill Place, Makeney

1791
Unlisted

A double-fronted house originally with a stockinger's shop on the north side built by Zephaniah Brown and subsequently converted to three houses. Two further small houses were added on the south side in 1823 by Z Brown junior. These houses were purchased by Anthony Radford Strutt in 1836 for £280. A pump stands nearby.

Forge Steps, nos. 1–5 (consecutive), Makeney

c.1750
Unlisted

Built of small bricks as a terrace c.1750 by the ironmaster Walter Mather for his workers. The doorways are shallow arched and the windows have sashes of a later date. These houses are illustrated at the top of this page.

Makeney Yard, nos. 1–4 (consecutive), Makeney Road, formerly Johnson's Buildings.

Eighteenth century
Listed Grade II

This block was originally a farm of considerable antiquity (possibly 15th century) and stabling. It is built of sandstone ashlar with an old tiled roof. It was partially rebuilt in 1732 after a fire. The Strutts purchased it in 1806 and converted it into four houses.

Makeney Terrace, nos. 1–8 (consecutive), Makeney Road

c.1820
Listed Grade II

This was built by the Strutts as a terrace of back-to-back stone houses. It has a hipped slate roof with moulded stone eaves and is two storeys in height.

The Bridge

Milford Dyehouse, Derby Road

1832
Listed Grade II

It is said to have been built in 1832, two years after William Strutt's death and though he may not have supervised its construction it is clearly a late development of his methods of fire-proofing. It is L-shaped, is built of coursed stone and has a hipped slate roof. The interior is of a vaulted construction with brick floors above. It has iron beams and cast iron columns linked by wrought iron tie rods. The building is eight bays long and two asymmetrical bays wide. The eastern facade has seven pairs of iron-framed windows each with a centre casement. It has double loading doors.

In a recess on the south wall, where the 'Turkey Red' building once stood, has been placed the mill bell dated 1781. To the east of this are re-erected columns from the demolished building.

Canteen at Milford Dyehouse, Derby Road

c.1800
Listed Grade II

It was built c.1800 and may well have been designed as an 'eating' room. It is a plain building, built of coursed stone with chamfered corners on the ground floor and has a slate roof.

Chimney at Milford Dyehouse, Derby Road

Late nineteenth century
Listed Grade II

This tall round brick mill chimney dominated the site. It was built in the late 19th century, replacing an earlier one that already existed in 1832.

South of the bridge

Derby Road, Mount Pleasant, nos. 1 and 2

1672 with later additions
Listed Grade II

Dated 1672 double-fronted, of coursed stone with mullioned windows most of which have been replaced by 19th century mullions.

Derby Road, Milford House

c.1792
Listed Grade II

A large ashlar stone house standing on embanked grounds built for Jedediah Strutt, who lived here briefly before moving to Derby. The main elevation facing east is of a symmetrical design. The building is two storeys high and has a slate roof and sash windows. The central round-arched doorway has an entablature with pilasters.

Derby Road, Moscow Cottages

By 1829
Listed Grade II

These were built as one building in the early nineteenth century, but in a 17th century style, to house farm workers.

Sunny Hill

Sunny Hill, no. 4

c.1813
Listed Grade II

The former 'Royal Oak' public house was built in the early 19th century of three storeys in coursed stone with brick chimneys and with later tiled roof and a symmetrical facade. Anthony Radford Strutt purchased it in 1847. It has 'Strutt' adjustable iron gutter brackets and cast iron windows within timber frames.

Sunny Hill, nos. 7 and 9

c.1792
Listed Grade II

These two-storey houses were built by Henry Reeder c.1792 and sold to the Strutts in 1808.

Sunny Hill, nos 13-37, formerly Sunny Hill Place

c.1791, 1807-22, 1823-24
Unlisted

Tradition has it that these houses served as a barracks - a residence for unmarried workers living away from home. It is of brick construction on the west side but stone on the east. The lower side is of three storeys and the upper of two. It was begun in 1791 when a single house was built by Thomas Sims. A further 11 houses were added between 1807 and 1822 by John Farnsworth and four more in 1823-24. Anthony Radford Strutt purchased this property in 1831 to accommodate small families.

Sunny Hill, nos 13-27

Sunny Hill, no. 45

1807
Unlisted

Built by John Bates for Edward Marson and purchased by the Strutts in 1856.

Sunny Hill, no. 47

1808
Listed Grade II

A two-storey double-pile stone house, gable end onto the road, built as a house and shop by John Bates for William Cash, a joiner. It was purchased by the Strutts in 1856.

Sunny Hill, no 47

Chevin Road and Well Lane

Chevin Alley, nos. 1–5 (consecutive)

c.1792
Listed Grade II

Strutt's terrace built c.1792 is an early example of sloping roof construction of three storeys in coursed stone, with slate roof and brick chimneys. Each house has a single room on each floor lit by a single window. Number 1 adjoins the mill buildings and the extension to the front was added in the 20th century for the village post office.

Chevin Road, nos 7–17, and 2 Sunny Hill (formerly Hazelwood Place)

1791-1813
Listed Grade II

12 dwellings built by William Marriott between 1791 and 1813 which included butcher's, baker's and stockinger's shops and a public house. Purchased by Anthony Radford Strutt in 1833 for £1,320, the Strutts later converted the public house into a reading room for the use of Milford residents.

Well Lane, nos. 8–14 (consecutive)

1792-96
Listed Grade II

A two-storey terrace in coursed stone built by the Strutts between 1792 and 1796. It has a hipped slate roof in diminishing courses, brick chimneys and sash windows. The stone wall on the eastern side of the street contains a recess for a pump. Cast iron launders were fitted to these houses in 1820.

Chevin Road, nos. 4 and 6, once known as 'The Bleach Houses'.

1792-1796
Listed Grade II

Originally a row of eight built for the bleach mill management by the Strutts. They are of two and a half storeys in height with brick chimneys. They are seen at their best from across the valley. This elevation reveals their superior status.

Chevin Road, Banks Buildings, nos. 1–16 (formerly called Bank Buildings)

1792-96 and 1911
Unlisted

A terrace of two-storey houses in coursed stone built by the Strutts between 1792 and 1796. The terrace was demolished three houses at a time and rebuilt as double-fronted houses with entries in 1911.

Chevin Road, Banks Buildings, formerly Bank Buildings, nos. 18-21 (consecutive)

c.1820
Unlisted

A stone built terrace, c.1820, built by the Strutts. Twenty years later the rear gardens of these houses were reduced to make room for the railway line.

Farms and Community Buildings

Derby Road, Moscow Farm

1812-15
Listed Grade II*

The farm was built by the Strutt family to supply produce to their workforce. The large, planned steading, largely constructed in gritstone with Welsh slate or Staffordshire plain tiled roofs, is enclosed by perimeter walls.

The principal original building consists of a T-shaped two-storey block that included a stable, cart sheds, feed preparation area and first floor storage. Two attached cow-houses form single-storey wings. On the south side of the cow-house was a large fold yard; a second large yard is enclosed to the north of the T-shaped block, which incorporates two forms of fire-proof construction. The first floor is carried on brick jack-arches springing from iron skewback beams - a form of floor construction paralleled in contemporary mills and warehouses built by the Strutts, and the first floor ceiling consisting of groined brick vaults without structural iron. Shortly after constructing the steading an L-shaped extension to the east cow-house and a linear extension to the west cow-house

were added in the same style. About 1830 the west cow-house was further extended so that it too formed an L-shape. An open-fronted range, possibly intended as calving pens, was constructed within the fold yard at about the same time. In the last quarter of the 19th century, the domestic accommodation was extended by converting part of the fire-proof block and adding a single-bay east extension. An open-fronted hay barn was constructed at the same time to replace storage space lost in the conversion. A number of minor buildings and additions date from the late 19th and early 20th centuries.

Makeney Road, Redhill Farm

1833
Listed Grade II

The farm is an interesting example of the multi-functional Strutt building. The range of farm buildings is constructed of coursed stone. Two segmental arches in the north elevation probably served cart-sheds. There are stables and cow-sheds with rectangular vents and a loft above. The adjoining building, Redhill Cottage, the earliest part of which is probably 17th century, has been altered probably in the late 18th or early 19th century. It appears to have been in separate occupation from the farm since it was purchased in 1833.

Derby Road, The William IV Public House, The Bridge, now the Milford Inn

c.1830
Listed Grade II

Built on land purchased by Hutton, the local surveyor and architect and probably built by him, it has three storeys and five bays. All the window openings are intact but some of the glazing is modern.

Derby Road, Milford Ebenezer Methodist Church

Listed Grade II
1846 and 1859

Built as a beerhouse and grocery by George Brassington and known as the Durham Ox, it was later sold to a religious group. It is dated 1846 (front) and 1859 (back and porch) and is built of coursed stone with moulded stone eaves.

Chevin Road, Milford County Junior Mixed and Infant School

c.1819-23
Listed Grade II

It is believed that this is the structure on which the Strutts spent nearly £3000 between c.1819 and 1823. There is some architectural evidence that it was built in two parts to serve two different functions.

It was constructed on a sloping site with the upper floor at street level (on the west side) and with an arched ground floor at the rear lower level (on the east side).

It is said that the ground floor was used for the Strutts' wagons and carts in the dye yard and the upper floor as a school. When the 'half-time' system was operating a gate in the mill yard allowed the children to move freely between the mill and the school. It is all now a school though the water tanks for the dyehouse are still under the school yard.

Built of coursed stone it has a slate roof with large cowl ventilators and multi-pane cast iron windows. The interior has very light iron roof trusses dated 1875.

Chevin Road, former Wesleyan Chapel

1842
Listed Grade II

It was built in 1842 of coursed stone of two storeys on a high plinth with a hipped slate roof and with sash windows with glazing bars. The entrance has been altered. The main facade is symmetrical.

Chevin Road, Milford Baptist Chapel

1849
Listed Grade II

It is dated 1849 on the facade. It is built of coursed stone with a high rusticated stone plinth and has a hipped slate roof. The design is symmetrical about a central entrance.

Shaw Lane, Milford Methodist Chapel

1823-25
Unlisted

The plan for this building is dated 1823. It is built of brick with a symmetrical front.

Derby Road, Holy Trinity Church

1846-48
Listed Grade II

It was built between 1846 and 1848 and designed by H Moffat on a site given by the Strutts. It is designed in the early English style and is built of coursed stone rubble with a tiled roof.

Water Power at Milford

Foundry Lane, Hopping Mill Weir adjacent to Glow Worm Foundry,

Present form 1799-1801
Listed Grade II

This weir is thought to be pre-Strutt but to have been altered by them substantially when they built their first cotton mill in Milford. It has a stone paved sloping surface and a concave curve upstream. The weir served three sites; on the north side a corn mill and a fulling mill and, via a goyt (water channel) on the south side, Strutt's printing mill and bleach works; and, south of the bridge, the main cotton mill site.

Makeney Road, Weir near the former Forge Mill,

c. 1790
Listed Grade II

The northern or upstream weir of the two south of the bridge was built some time between 1787 and 1792 and is believed to have been constructed by the Strutts.

The lower weir was constructed some time before 1840, In its centre is a stone fish ladder.

Transport Features at Milford

Derby Road, Milford Bridge

1793
Listed Grade II

The river bridge was built in 1793 by Jedediah Strutt. It is ashlar with two segmental arches and with rusticated outwaters. A parapet cantilevered out was added in 1906.

Chevin Road, the Northern and Southern Entrance Arches to the Milford Railway Tunnel

1840
Listed Grade II

Southern entrance

The tunnel was constructed in 1840 for the North Midland Railway Company, the first large tunnel on the line to be built. The engineers were George and Robert Stephenson. The entrances have a series of decreasing semi-circular concentric stone arches. The tunnel is still in use.

The Tower, Sunny Hill, Milford

1839
Listed Grade II

The Tower, square in plan, is sited over the railway tunnel. It is four storeys in height and has openings on each floor. It was built by the North Midland Railway Company when the section of the line between Derby and Belper, which opened in 1840, was being constructed. For many years it was believed that the tower had served as a siting tower to survey the line, however, recent research suggests that it was in fact a semaphore tower and was used to display signals to indicate to engine drivers using the tunnel whether the line was clear.

Peckwash Mill, Little Eaton

The relationship between papermaking and the textile industry is an area of study which needs closer investigation. Within the Derwent Valley there were paper mills associated with two of the major cotton spinning sites, Masson and Darley Abbey and at least three others within, or adjacent to, the nominated site. On the one hand cotton waste was a raw material for the paper mills; on the other, the thread manufacturers and hosiery warehouses used large quantities of paper for packaging their products, for wrapping parcels to be dispatched to customers, and for administrative purposes. The Strutts from 1835 and the Evans' both had their own printing departments.

On this site, Thomas Tempest, 1768-1832, a corn miller developed an extensive paper mill. The building which survives is now a dwelling. It is built of coursed stone and was erected c.1800. It is similar in design to an Arkwright generation cotton spinning mill, long and relatively narrow. The mill was powered by water from the river Derwent and this was channelled into a series of goyts to drive several water wheels located within the mill structure itself, and on the east side. Subsequently, two turbines housed in a separate building replaced the water wheels. This building, now a garage, has an eastern bay of brick-arched and iron fire-proof construction.

Steam power was introduced to the site c.1890 and the large brick chimney which still dominates the area was built at this time. This proved to be the undoing of the paper manufactory. In 1906 a neighbour successfully sued the company on grounds of smoke and pollution and in 1908 the enterprise was forced to close. Other businesses used the site until the 1960s after which the mill became derelict. In 1990 it was converted into a single residence. The building retains its original form and the rest of the site has been landscaped as a garden. The mill goyts and wheelpits have been exposed and

as a result much of the archaeology of the site can now be interpreted.

To the east of the mill, on the hill, is a terrace of fourteen cottages built for the paper mill c.1850; some are two storeys and some three storeys.

Darley Abbey

The settlement of Darley Abbey lies a little over 2 kilometres north of Derby City Centre. By the 17th century this small settlement had become established as an industrial hamlet near, but quite separate from, Derby. By the middle of the century there were two fulling mills and two corn mills and there may also have been a forge, Shrogg's forge. By the 1680s the fulling mills had grown to three and 30 years later a paper mill had been added. From c.1750 one of the more distinguished of these industrial tenants was William Duesbury, 1725-1786, the founder of the Derby Porcelain Factory, who had a flint mill here. In the early 1770s there were five separate water-powered mills; a paper mill, a corn mill, a flint mill, a china mill and a leather mill.

It was to this well established industrial settlement that the Evans family added their cotton mill development in 1782 and subsequently their factory village.

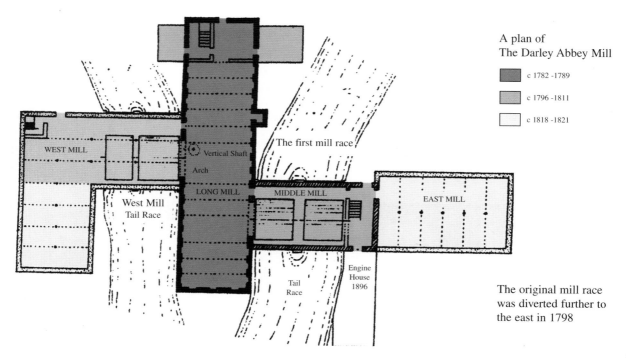

A plan of
The Darley Abbey Mill

■ c 1782 -1789

▨ c 1796 -1811

□ c 1818 -1821

The original mill race was diverted further to the east in 1798

The Boar's Head Mills

The cotton mill structures which survive in Darley Abbey are among the most complete of any of the early cotton factory sites and, in the context of the Derwent Valley, are comparable with Cromford in the degree to which both the principal and the ancillary buildings remain intact.

A detailed survey of the site is underway and the conclusions recorded here are subject to further evaluation.

Long Mill

1782-89
Listed Grade II

The mill in its present form was re-built in 1789 after fire in December 1788 destroyed the earlier building of 1782. It is likely that the existing structure incorporates parts of the shell of the first mill but no detailed examination of the mill which could confirm the extent to which this may be true has been made.

The five-storey plus attic mill is 38.4 metres long and 10.1 metres wide externally and has a masonry ground floor with brick above. Many of the exposed wooden structural members inside the mill are protected against fire by metal sheathing. It is not clear whether this is contemporary with the re-building. If it is an original feature of 1789, it is probably the earliest surviving example of fire-proofing in a textile mill.

To the left, Long Mill; to the right, the West Mill

The roof is framed by wooden queen post trusses with metal cladding and the collars of the trusses are cambered to give a central headroom of over six feet. There are short side walls below the lower rank of purlins and these are also metal-sheeted while the roof slopes above the purlins are plastered on wooden lathes. There is a plaster partition with

a panel door dividing off a section of the attic and this may be the Sunday School meeting room referred to in a letter of 1791 from Evans to the Royal Exchange Insurance Company. The attic was reputedly used as a schoolroom and its height and finish would allow such use. A similar use is known to have been made of the Belper North Mill roof space.

The attic floor is supported by a matrix of wooden beams, an arrangement quite different from any of the lower floors. The matrix is formed of transverse members every two bays (the tie-beams of the trusses) with four longitudinal members between and the beams are all clad in sheet metal. The irregularly spaced cast iron columns are secondary and thus this top floor was probably a clear space.

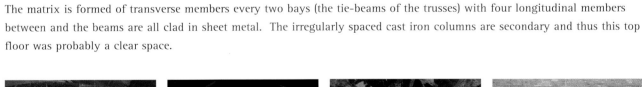

The floor below, in contrast, has a transverse beam each bay with a central rank of cruciform cast iron columns augmented by later round section cast iron columns. It is not clear that these columns are original, and taking into account the date of the reconstruction of the mill it is likely that they were added later. In July 1799 the Griffin Foundry in Chesterfield supplied 23 'iron pillars' but it is not clear which part of the mill these were for.

Among the external features of Long Mill are a number of different window designs. It is known that the structure was first equipped with opening casements which were later mostly replaced by sash windows. On the eastern elevation of the mill a number of wooden multi-paned windows with cast iron opening casements survive and it is likely that these are some of the original windows. Casements were still being purchased in 1793 from the Griffin Foundry in Chesterfield who also supplied iron sashes in 1798. Other iron casements came from Bassetts of Ashbourne.

A plan made by Benjamin Outram for the extension of the Derby Canal to Darley Abbey dated 1792 indicates that the mill was served by a cut from the river which ran to the east of the building. The line of this cut was altered some time after 1825 probably to allow for the development of further building to the North of the site. The middle mill is thought to have been constructed between 1796 and 1801. Its lowest storey housed two water wheels, one of which is known to have been a flood wheel, that is to say a wheel set at a higher elevation so that it could be used when the river was running above its usual level. This wheel, built of timber, together with its wheelhouse, cost £791 and was completed in 1797. A second new wheel was constructed in 1804-05. By 1811 Long Mill had also been extended to the West by the addition of a new wing served by its own cut from the river.

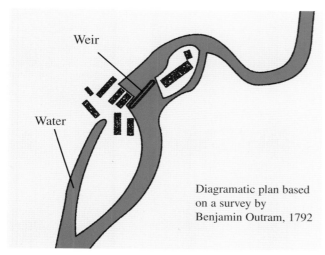

Weir

Water

Diagramatic plan based on a survey by Benjamin Outram, 1792

West Mill and East Mill

1819-21
Listed Grade II

It is known that the Evans' extended their mill again in 1818 and finally in 1821. It would appear from the mill records that between 1819 and 1821 both the East new mill and the West new mill were under construction. In 1819 alone more than £3,000 was spent on the East Mill and nearly £4,700 on the West Mill. The building works continued into 1821 and a new waterwheel was purchased during the year at a cost of £1,750. It is not clear whether this wheel was for the West Mill or was a further replacement wheel for the Middle Mill to serve the new East Mill.

The West Mill is of particular interest. It is an L-shaped extension projecting from the middle five bays of Long Mill. Like Long Mill it is brick-built with a masonry ground floor but it is a storey lower and a passage leads from the fourth floor of Long Mill through a hip-slope to the roof space of West Mill.

The entire extension is fire-proof with brick jack arches running longitudinally in the link block and transversely in the return, thus maintaining a single alignment of vaulting. The cast iron skewbacks are supported by round cast iron columns three to each of the longitudinal beams in the link and one to each of the transverse beams of the return.

It is not known when the cut which supplied the two wheels housed in the West Mill wheelpits was constructed.

A detailed investigation of the East Mill has yet to be undertaken.

The Boar's Head Mills north of the road

From 1790
Listed Grade II

This part of the mill site has not been surveyed but it is clear from documentary and visual evidence that parts of it date from the 1790s and most of the remainder from the early years of the 19th century. A plan of 1846 confirms this impression. The buildings include an office block, managerial housing, stabling (1804-05), warehousing, gassing sheds and a mill which appears to have always derived its power from a steam engine. This structure may at one time have been used in part as a dye house and is thought to have been built in the 1820s.

The Kiosk-Gatehouse

Before 1846
Listed Grade II

An octagonal kiosk stands at the entrance to the mill yard. It is similar (though smaller) to the gatehouse which has survived at Stanley Mills near Perth, and which served the same purpose. A gatehouse once stood inside the entrance to the Cromford Mills and also at Wedgwood's factory at Etruria. Indeed the gatehouse was as much part of the early factory as the factory bell.

In Darley Abbey the gatehouse has for so long served as a tollhouse that it has come to assume that name but its earlier function is clear from its location.

The Darley Abbey cotton mills, north and south of the road and the other industrial sites c.1850.

Housing in Darley Abbey

The settlement the Evans created in Darley Abbey has survived almost intact. Many of the houses have been altered externally and internally, for the most part superficially, and the privies and pigsties have gone. But few significant buildings other than the two Evans' houses, Darley House and Darley Hall, the Evans' farm and the paper mill, have been demolished. It is in no sense a planned or model community having grown incrementally as land became available over at least 50 years and this is the only pattern which is discernible in its growth. But as an early factory village, in its range of properties and house types, it is no less important than Belper or Cromford.

Like the other Derwent Valley factory masters the Evans' provided houses for their mill workers. They acquired a number of houses when they purchased the existing mills in Darley Abbey and some of these were pressed into service to accommodate the first mill families. It is not clear when they began to build their own housing either in Darley Abbey or in the neighbouring settlement of Allestree where they also had factory housing for the Darley Abbey Mills. Plainly, a number of houses were available by 1787 when they advertised for labour in the Derby Mercury offering "comfortable houses with every convenience at Darley or Allestry [sic]". An unofficial census a year later recorded the total number of houses in Darley Abbey as 47, which gives some idea of the size of the settlement at that time and provides a basis against which to measure subsequent growth.

The Square (Flat Square)

Before 1792
Nos. 1-12 Listed Grade II

West Row Listed Grade II

This was probably the first of the housing development provided by the Evans'. The houses were built on a flat piece of land just over the bridge from the cotton mills. As the name suggests, they are built round three sides of a square and are three-storeyed, brick-built with slate roofs and one continuous roof line.

The houses to the north and south of the square are larger than those on the west and face into the square. Those on the west face outwards and the kitchen extensions face into the square. The north-south houses contained about 53.3 square metres internally when first built. Those at the rear of the square, on the west, in contrast, were approximately half the size at 27.3 square metres.

Darley Street

Date Unconfirmed
Nos. 5-10 listed Grade II

Darley Street includes four three-storeyed pairs of cottages, three on the western side and one on the east. Brick built with slate roofs, they are similar in size to the larger houses in The Square.

Hill Square

Date Unconfirmed
Unlisted

This square is formed by blocks of houses of which some are back-to-back. Built in brick and slate-roofed they are mostly of two storeys. On the west side the block of three is believed to have been built originally as six back-to-back houses.

On the south side there are blocks of four houses and three houses, and between them the two houses which are larger and very much later in construction.

Poplar Row

Before 1823
Listed Grade II

A row of five three-storey, brick and slate houses. They occupy the level ground at the bottom of New Road. They are thought to be the houses built by the Evans' between 1819 and 1823 referred to in the company ledger as "five houses built by the riverside".

Lower New Road

Before 1826
Unlisted

Three-storey brick and slate houses built in the form of cluster houses in two blocks of four with gardens to the side and rear, at the bottom of New Road. They all have later extensions.

Upper New Road

Before 1826
Unlisted

This group of two blocks in the cluster house format comprises eight houses in all. The blocks are brick-built with slate roofs and the elevations have been given an unusual elegance for mill workers' housing, the doors being set in blank arched recesses. The road-side elevation is stuccoed and painted but the quality of the original brickwork is evident at the rear.

The houses to the rear have allotment gardens. No evidence remains of ancillary buildings to house privies or pigsties, though there is ample space for there to have been such facilities. The care with which these blocks have been designed is thought to be attributable to their high visibility from the Evans' residence.

The Hollies/White House

The Hollies 1803-06
The White House Date Unconfirmed
The White House Listed Grade II

The Hollies is a large house built in brick and slate attached to a larger house, the White House, which was built later. These substantial dwellings were used as managers' houses and the White House was the home of John Peacock who purchased the cotton mills after Walter Evans' death in 1903.

Brick Row

1797-98 and 1798-1800
Listed Grade II

Brick Row, which is brick-built with slate roofs, today comprises 14 three-storeyed houses. It has the appearance of a single terrace; in fact it was constructed in two phases, described in the Evans ledgers as five houses and a schoolroom, 1797-98, and eight houses and a schoolroom, 1798-1800. The former schoolrooms were at second floor level over the houses that are now numbered 6-12 Brick Row. Internal evidence of the construction confirms this interpretation and externally it can be seen that the second floor windows of these houses are not aligned over those below. The schoolrooms were later sub divided to create additional bedroom space for the houses below; also, certain of the houses in both phases were sub divided or amalgamated.

Most of the windows and doors in the row have been altered, but a few early cast iron casements set into larger wooden-paned frames have survived; for example at no. 11. The house at the northern end of the row, no.16, once had its entrance door on the main terrace frontage. This was repositioned when the end bay was added.

Allotments for each house were provided on the other side of the road. The house at the northern end of the row was adapted to give it the appearance of a lodge for Darley House whose main drive was opposite.

The Four Houses

1792
Unlisted

These four houses are built of brick and slate in the cluster house form and contain three storeys. Each house was originally 45 square metres internally. They were completed in 1792, an early experiment with the cluster house format, later to be adopted by Charles Bage in Shrewsbury and by William Strutt in Belper. Unlike the Belper cluster houses they do not have private gardens or pigsties, though they were provided with "necessaries" (lavatories) in 1796. They each had an allotment on land behind the Mile Ash houses.

The unlisted lower terrace

The listed terrace of 12 houses

Mile(s) Ash Lane

1795-96
Listed Grade II

The upper single stepped terrace of 12 houses was built in 1795-96. It contains three storeys and is built of brick and slate and each house in the terrace was provided with a lavatory and a pigsty together with a plot of land to the rear. The lower terrace, illustrated above, was in existence by 1871.

Lavender Row

Date Unconfirmed
Listed Grade II

This is the terrace in Darley Abbey which gives the greatest impression of quality in construction and design. It is of three storeys and built in brick and slate with a stepped roof line to accommodate the slope. Architectural distinction is provided by the lintels over the windows and doors having projecting keystones. Each house had a lavatory and a plot of land to the rear.

Folly Houses

Date Unconfirmed
Unlisted

These houses are on the other side of the river from the main village. Thomas Evans acquired the site in 1778 possibly with a view to using the adjoining stream of water to power a mill. When this proved impossible the houses were added to the Evans' housing stock. Two of the original three houses remain.

Houses in Mill Yard

c.1800
Listed Grade II

Five houses were built within the perimeter of the cotton mill site. They were constructed at different times as the mill expanded and were occupied by foremen at the mill or at the adjoining bleaching and dye works. The houses reflect the status of their occupiers, being larger than most of the other houses in the settlement.

St Matthew's Church

1818
Listed Grade C

Designed by Moses Wood of Nottingham (Built by Walter Evans in 1818). It is described by Pevsner as "unaisled, of Commissioners' type with tall slender windows with Perpendicular tracery and angle pinnacles". The square tower at the west end is also pinnacled. The crypt beneath the altar contains the remains of nine members of the Evans family, together with those of Moses Harvey, a junior partner in the cotton mill. The Churchyard has ornate cast iron gates of impressive size; many of the slate headstones were provided by the Evans' for their workers.

Darley Abbey School

1826
Listed Grade II

Designed by Moses Wood of Nottingham and built in 1826 as a school room with houses for the Master and Mistress at each end. Red-brick, two storeys, the windows to the ground storey are round-headed and in round-headed recesses; there is a sill band to the first floor and a stone cornice; there are pediments to the ends (which project slightly), a pediment in the centre with a clock and plain wrought iron railings enclosing a small playground at either end. It was endowed by Walter Evans who left £8,000 in his will to be invested for the teaching of poor children aged four to twelve in the parish "and not more than 40 at a time".
The building is now in use as offices.

Derby

Derby Silk Mill

1721, Rebuilt 1910
Listed Grade II

Derby Silk Mill lies besides the river Derwent, on the north-eastern edge of the city centre. Today, it has a surprisingly tranquil setting, given its location within an urban environment. Relatively little remains of the original physical structure of Lombe's Mill.

The massive stone arches that provided the foundations of the eastern side of the five-storey "Italian Works", as Lombe's Mill was known, can still be seen running along the western bank of the river Derwent. The remainder of the old mill was destroyed by fire in 1910 and rebuilt three storeys high. The adjacent stair tower on the south-western corner of the building, perhaps its most distinctive architectural feature, was rebuilt using the original bricks, together with the nineteenth century belfry.

The courtyard on the western side of the building was originally occupied by the mill race. The course of the flume, which carried the water back to the river Derwent, can still be seen within the landscaped gardens to the south of the mill.

The early industrial buildings which adjoined the mill on the northern side, including the first silk mill and town corn mills, have disappeared, and their place is now occupied by a brick extension that is contemporary with the present mill building.

Wrought Iron Gates

1725
Listed Grade II

The original wrought iron gates made for the mill in 1725 by the renowned Derbyshire craftsman, Robert Bakewell, have been restored and now stand at the entrance to a courtyard on the western side of the mill building at 90 degrees to their original position.

3b History and Development

It is now more than 30 years since the late Professor J D Chambers described the Derwent Valley as the "cradle of the new factory system". It is an accolade which has stood the test of critical analysis, further research and reflection. It was here in the Derwent Valley that the essential ingredients of factory production were successfully combined. A source of power, in this case water power, was applied to a series of complex mechanised processes for the first time on a relatively large scale. Not only was textile production revolutionised with dramatic consequences for the British economy, the Arkwright model also informed and inspired developments in other industries.

Why these developments should have happened in the Derwent Valley, rather than in any one of numerous locations endowed by nature with a reasonable water supply, is a question to which there may be no single answer. The natural potential of the river Derwent, at first sight a powerful element in the story, is on closer examination less a determining influence in the first steps of this chain of events than might be anticipated. The water power requirements of the early initiatives in Derby and in Cromford were so small, a large source of water power would have been an embarrassment. So in Derby, Lombe used the town corn mill weir and leats; and in Cromford, Arkwright positioned his first mill on a lead mine drainage channel and a modest brook. The later developments in Belper, Milford and Darley Abbey and at Masson Mill, were on a larger scale: by this time, it was worth investing substantially in the engineering solutions required to tame the volatility of the river and so enjoy the massive power it could provide.

What other factors should be taken into account? Lombe had lived in Derby and had local connections. and recent research suggests the town's leading citizens wanted the silk mill established there. It is known that Arkwright sought a reliable source of water but he was also attracted by the easy availability of child labour in and around Cromford, where the lead mining industry offered little scope for the employment of young children. He also needed to be near the hosiery centres of Derby and Nottingham where he expected to sell his yarn.

This market horizon was also the boundary within which Arkwright's financial sponsors - Samuel Need from Nottingham and Jedediah Strutt from Derby - were prepared to operate.

The problem they sought to resolve was widely recognised. Demand for yarn had outstripped supply and while Hargreaves' Jenny offered a significant increase in output over hand-spinning, it was a relatively complicated machine to operate and not suitable for child labour. The Arkwright frame and the family of devices which followed it were, in contrast, all of a scale and simplicity of operation as to be suitable for young people.

Sir Richard did not achieve all his objectives. Some processes eluded even his mechanical skill. He had to persevere with hand picking and cleaning his raw cotton: the devices he had patented for this purpose did not work. But even where hands had to replace machines in the Arkwright system, he ensured the smooth delivery from one process to the next. Stanley Chapman sees this as the essence of Arkwright's achievement: "The novel requirement was co-ordinating and managerial skill rather than the traditional artisan technology". Once the Arkwright system had been established it was the absence or scarcity of such skills which as much as any other factor determined the rate at which the system was disseminated. Those who mastered the new spinning system found they possessed skills which were much in demand. It was through these custodians of the new technology that the Arkwright system was propagated at home and abroad.

By 1782-84 it was clear that Arkwright's patents were at risk, and after 1785, all restrictions had been set aside. Investment opportunities in the new industry, which had been confined to Arkwright, his partners and his licensees (and some who operated outside the law), now became available to a wide spectrum of investors, opportunists and would-be entrepreneurs. By 1788, Chapman's figures suggest no less than 208 Arkwright-type mills were in existence in Great Britain and there were four mills in France and five in Germany. There were also a number of mills in Ireland. Already the development which had begun so tentatively in Cromford in 1771 had instigated widespread cultural and economic change.

Our inheritance from the Derwent factory masters, Richard Arkwright, Jedediah Strutt, Peter Nightingale and Thomas Evans, also includes some of the first examples of factory housing and of industrial communities. These are not model villages in the sense that they were pre-planned or built to a known blue-print but they soon became models for other community builders within Great Britain and abroad. Within these social units the factory master (later it would be more accurate to use the word squire) was almost as much in control of the residents in their homes as he was of his workforce in the mills. The social controls which are most obvious in Belper, the tied houses, the fines for misbehaviour at work and in the street, the watchmen, the payments in truck and the more subtle influences associated with food and welfare provision, were no doubt in use in Cromford and Darley Abbey in a similar if not identical form. But the documentary evidence of life in these communities has not survived to the degree it has for Belper and Milford.

Derby: the Silk Mill

The story of how the large-scale manufacturing of high quality silk thread arrived in Derby early in the eighteenth century is now very much better understood thanks to recent research by Anthony Calladine. It is clear there were several crucial factors and these include the driving enthusiasm and inventive genius of a few key individuals.

Silk making in late seventeenth century England had grown during a period when fashion demanded luxury silk items, a demand which was met, in part, by the Huguenot refugees from France who settled in England, many of whom were skilled silk weavers.

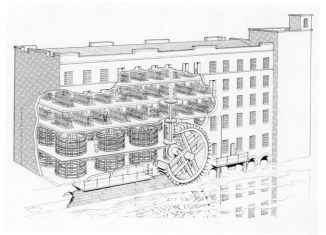

A conjectural reconstruction of Lombes Silk Mill

At the end of the seventeenth century, Thomas Cotchett, a middle-aged Derby solicitor, became interested in the commercial possibilities of silk manufacture using water-powered machinery. He turned to George Sorocold, an engineer who had recently been commissioned to supply Derby with piped water, to build him a water-powered mill on an island in the Derwent near the centre of Derby. Cotchett installed a number of "Dutch machines" but the project was not a success because, according to a contemporary witness, it was inadequately equipped. The experiment might have ended here but one of Cotchett's employees, John Lombe, was determined to take things further. He was convinced that if the secret Italian process could be introduced to the country there would be a large market for the high quality silk it would produce. Lombe carried out a daring piece of industrial espionage, and returned to England with a number of Italian workmen and detailed drawings of the Piedmontese throwing machines. In 1718 Thomas Lombe was granted a 14 year patent, and in 1721 he and his brother began to build a mill adjacent to Cotchett's mill and as a near neighbour of the Derby corn mill. Calladine suggests that Lombe had been actively encouraged to set up his mill in Derby by some of the town's most prominent citizens who were anxious to secure a new industry for the neighbourhood.

The Italian machines did not require a large power source to drive them and Lombe's mill was served by a single undershot wheel 7m in diameter and probably about 1.8m broad. The mill used the weir and tail-race of the town corn mill, though the weir may have been raised.

The mill was five storeys high, 33.5m long and 12m wide.

The storeys were supported on stone arches which allowed the river Derwent when in flood to pass through them. A shallow pitched roof was concealed behind a parapet and the building was equipped with large sash windows 1.8m high and 0.96m wide. A second building, the doubling shop, was constructed in line with the mill. This contained the doubling machinery which was all hand powered. There was also a warehouse and service space which included a carpenter's room and the mill offices.

Lombe's mill contained many elements of the modern factory. The machinery was driven from a common power source and housed in a large multi-storeyed building. A large labour force was employed - by 1730, 300 people are said to have been at work in this enterprise - and there is some indication that the mill may have had a form of hot-air heating system similar to those found later in the Arkwright cotton mills.

The Lombe experiment was copied in Stockport, Macclesfield, Congleton and elsewhere, but only at Congleton was a mill built on a similar scale. Thirty years after the expiry of Lombe's patent only seven mills had been built; though a very much larger number were manufacturing tram, a lower quality product.

Lombe's achievements

The significance of Lombe's achievements should not be measured wholly in terms of the growth and extent of the mechanised silk throwing industry stimulated by his example. The silk industry was never destined to serve a large market. Of greater importance by far was the system of working and the organisation of the labour force around the rigid demands of a common power source which the Derby mill bequeathed. As the Strutts made clear, it was an inheritance the later factory masters well understood. The degree to which Lombe's mill offered succeeding generations an example of mill design is more difficult to assess. Was it a coincidence that Masson Mill as it was first built, had a high parapet concealing a low pitched roof which gave it a striking similarity to the Derby Silk Mill? The first mill at Cromford may also have had a parapet to the roof judging from one early illustration, though this is not confirmed by other depictions. Certainly the first Cromford Mill followed the Silk Mill in adopting sash windows and, as has been pointed out, there is the possibility that the later mills might have borrowed an earlier heating system. There are, however, important differences.

The later cotton mills were built significantly narrower than Lombe's mill. Not having to accommodate such bulky machinery the extra width offered no advantage. There may also have been differences in the floor to ceiling heights.

Beyond this point comparison is unhelpful. The processes which are subsumed within the term "spinning" are, by comparison with throwing silk, so numerous and relatively more complicated that not even Richard Arkwright, as one of his contemporaries put it "allowed by all his acquaints to be a very ingenious man" was able, or the genius of William Strutt was sufficient, to mechanise every step of the passage of raw cotton to spun yarn. It was, however, for the degree to which he was successful that Richard Arkwright won the accolade "Father of the Factory System".

Cotton Mill, Cromford, 10th Dec. 1771.

WANTED immediately, two Journeymen Clock-Makers, or others that underſtands Tooth and Pinion well: Alſo a Smith that can forge and file.—Likewiſe two Wood Turners that have been accuſtomed to Wheel-making, Spoke-turning, &c. Weavers reſiding in this Neighbourhood, by applying at the Mill, may have good Work. There is Employment at the above Place, for Women, Children, &c. and good Wages.
N. B. A Quantity of Box Wood is wanted: Any Perſons whom the above may ſuit, will be treated with by Meſſrs. Arkwright and Co. at the Mill, or Mr. Strutt, in Derby.

Cromford

It was at Cromford that Richard Arkwright extended the range and scale of his mechanisation of cotton spinning and devised the factory production techniques which yoked machinery, the workforce and water power as they had never been harnessed before. In his hands the factory system evolved and matured, creating a model which was recognised and copied across the world.

First steps

Richard Arkwright's first steps in Cromford were slow and tentative. It is clear from a letter of March 1772, seven months after the lease at Cromford had been signed, that though he boasted to his partner Jedediah Strutt that he would be able to make "three frames in a fortnet" [sic] in reality, not a single frame had been made. Nor had the building been completed: the sash windows were still to be fitted and he was waiting for latches and door fittings. He was also still recruiting key staff and not finding it easy.

Apart from this glimpse of early difficulties, little is known of the first years of the new enterprise. To power the mill Richard Arkwright separated Cromford Sough from the Bonsall Brook and created a new watercourse to the mill probably taking it across the road by aqueduct. It is known from the details of a dispute with his landlord that the mill

Cromford Mill
Powered buildings and site development

1771

c. 1776

c. 1785

c. 1791

A conjectural diagram

was operational by 1774 but no further information is available. Much of his time in the early years in Cromford must have been taken up with experiment. Between 1772 and 1775 he perfected the mechanisation of the pre-spinning processes, the key elements of which were embodied in his second patent of 1775 and which he put into operation in his second Cromford Mill built in 1776-77.

To finance this venture Arkwright looked outside the partnership which had built the first mill and turned to Peter Nightingale, a wealthy lead merchant and neighbouring land owner. At a cost of £20,000, Nightingale took over the purchase of the Cromford Estate which Arkwright had negotiated and, perhaps as a reward to Arkwright, committed himself to building Arkwright a residence. The site they chose overlooked the mill. Rock House became Arkwright's home for the rest of his life. In a subsequent arrangement Nightingale provided Arkwright with £2,000 for the second Cromford Mill and a further £1,000 to build houses for the work people.

The housing Nightingale financed was in North Street and in 1780 a further £750 was paid for houses higher up Cromford Hill. There may well have been other financial arrangements to support buildings at the mill site or in the village as, for example, the construction of the "Black Greyhound" or "Black Dog" as the Greyhound Inn was first known; but no details have survived.

The Arkwright business empire is born

The development of the second Cromford Mill in 1776-77 was followed by a period of intense activity. In 1777 mills were built by Arkwright and his family at Birkacre, Bakewell and Wirksworth; at Rocester in 1781 and at Cressbrook in 1783. Between 1776 and 1781 his partner in the first Cromford Mill, Jedediah Strutt, built his first mills at Belper and at Milford. Elsewhere, royalty agreements licensing the use of Arkwright machinery allowed the Arkwright system to proliferate in addition to which there were those who pirated his machinery and operated outside the law.

Notwithstanding substantial expansion further afield, Arkwright continued to develop his mill enterprise at Cromford. There is more than a hint of major growth in 1781 when the mills advertised for:

> FORGING and Filing Smiths, Joiners and Carpenters, Framework-Knitters and Weavers, with large Families. Likewife Children of all Ages; above feven Years old, may have conftant Employment. Boys and young Men may have Trades taught them, which will enable them to maintain a Family in a fhort Time. Two or three young Men who can write a good Hand, are alfo wanted.
> By perfonal Application at the COTTON-MILLS, Particulars may be known.
> SEPTEMBER 19, 1781.

The Arkwright Inventions

The development of the Arkwright water frame made available the first continuous spinning process which could be operated by machine minders rather than skilled operatives.

Arkwright's first patent, which he obtained in July 1769, was for a machine which spun yarn by means of rollers, flyers and bobbins. The cotton was "drawn" by pairs of rollers, each successive pair moving faster than the

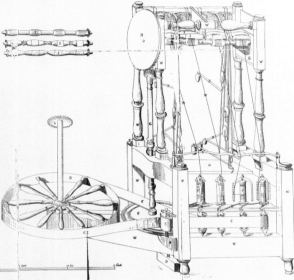

The Arkwright Frame illustrated in the first Patent

preceding one, with twist added by bobbins and flyers. The front pair of rollers was weighted by lead weights hooked over the top roller. This prevented the twist running back up the roving and forcing the rollers apart. The top roller was covered with leather and the bottom one fluted so that the cotton was held firmly as it passed between the two.

The production models used the basic drafting head shown in the patent drawing mounted side by side on a wooden frame and driven from a water wheel by gearing, wooden line shafting and belts.

Joseph Wright's portrait of Sir Richard shows his subject and, by his side, the invention on which his fame and fortune were based. In selecting the drafting head (the

roller device), as the icon of his subject's achievement, and in painting it so accurately, Joseph Wright demonstrated a genuine understanding of the Arkwright spinning process.

The production models of the water frame varied in size from four spindles to the ninety-six spindle machine, an example of which, from Cromford Mill, is preserved at the Helmshore Higher Mill Museum in Lancashire. The factory masters found it an advantage to have frames of more than one size so that they could produce yarns in varying degrees of thickness, known in the trade as counts, in appropriate quantities according to the demands of the market.

The 96 spindle Arkwright waterframe, originally from Cromford, preserved at Helmshore Higher Mill Museum

The eight spindle Arkwright waterframe, originally from Cromford, preserved in the Science Museum, London

Some of the elements of Arkwright's Second Patent 1775

Once Arkwright had successfully adapted his spinning machine to factory production, he turned his attention to the preparatory processes which precede spinning in the production of yarn. The need had become acute. Until carding and roving could be mechanised to keep pace with spinning, continuous production, the essence of the factory system, could not be achieved. Arkwright's solutions to these problems were set

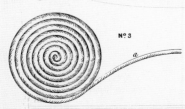

The Lap which was fed into the Carding Engine as shown in the patent drawing

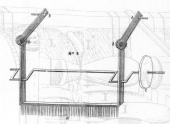

The Crank and Comb as shown in the patent drawing. Before the introduction of this device continuous carding was not possible with the result that other production processes were held up and the quality of the product was affected.

The Crank and Comb installed on the Arkwright Carding Engine, preserved in Bolton

A bobbin and flyer for the roving frame as shown in the patent drawing

carding machinery until the middle of the twentieth century. The Arkwright system, or "package" of processes has been, and remains, of the greatest significance to the world's textile industries. The improvements that Arkwright made to carding were ultimately applied to all textile fibres other than monofilaments and the modern machine is a recognisable descendent of Arkwright's first factory models. Roller drawing, too, had a wider application and was adapted to deal with other fibres. It remained a key component of the mule, of the throstle and of the ring frame, the most important devices by far in the spinning of cotton, wool, flax, jute and waste silk, as well as of chopped synthetic fibres.

out in his second patent which he obtained in 1775. This comprised a series of devices with which he addressed the technical problems of opening and cleaning the cotton; carding, a process by which all the fibres are laid parallel; and the creation of slivers and rovings, the loose, slightly twisted ropes of fibre which formed the raw material for the spinning frames.

By no means all Arkwright's solutions were effective. His attempts to mechanise opening and cleaning failed and these, the first stages in making ready the raw cotton, continued to be performed by hand until the 1790s when the first successful batting machines became available.

Overall his achievement was remarkable, both in its immediate affect and in its longevity. Some of Arkwright's inventions such as the crank and comb continued in use on

The international implications of Arkwright's inventions were wide-spread and extended beyond the immediate economic effects of technological transfer as the Arkwright system became established in countries outside Great Britain. The factory production of cotton yarn also led to cotton becoming the most important textile fibre in the world for a period of more than a century and the impact of large scale cultivation on countries such as the United States, Egypt and India was profound. The Arkwright system made possible the production of cheap clothing and household textiles for a wide cross-section of the population, improving comfort and personal hygiene.

An Arkwright drawing frame preserved at Helmshore Higher Mill Museum.

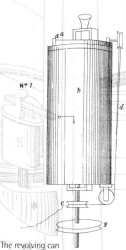

The revolving can to receive rovings as shown in the patent drawing. The can or lantern frame proved unreliable though the machine was manufactured and put into productive use.

The can frame preserved at the Helmshore Higher Mill Museum.

Original Timber line shafting preserved in Bolton

It has not yet proved possible to link this expansion to a particular building phase at Cromford.

In 1783 he turned his attention to Matlock Bath and to the construction of Masson Mill. This was built on land acquired in 1780 from the proprietors of the adjacent paper mill which had been erected in 1769. It is not known when Masson was first in production but it is likely to have been in time for the boom years of 1786-87.

After Sir Richard Arkwright's death in 1792, Richard Arkwright junior sold most of his remaining cotton mill interests outside Matlock Bath and Cromford. That he retained these mills may well have had more to do with their role in sustaining the Willersley Estate than their inherent profitability.

At Cromford the disputes over water rights which had rumbled on through the 1830s reached a conclusion in 1839 and, by 1847, when Thomas Carlyle visited the area, he was made aware the end was near. He wrote to his brother "the Mother of all the Mills [is] very nearly fallen silent now, likely soon to go out altogether".

The mills in decline

From the late 1820s profits from the Cromford and Masson Mills are likely to have been nominal and there are few indications of any attempt to improve their performance. In 1834 the Factories Inquiry recorded that water frames were still in use in the Arkwright Mill and 20 years later when the son of Johann Gottfried Brugelmann visited Masson he was amazed to see "the great inventor's machinery, mahoganied by age, is still at work.... after more than seventy years of toil".

The mills passed to Peter Arkwright 1784-1866 and on in turn to Frederic Arkwright 1806-74. The family earned universal acclaim locally for keeping the mills at work during the cotton famine in the early 1860s at considerable cost to themselves, but their patience was not infinite. In 1872 Frederic had both sites valued and came close to a sale. Only Masson had retained any value. No more than a small section of the Cromford Mill remained in use: a winding room; a blowing room; and a making up room. But it was left to his son, Frederic Charles Arkwright (1853-1923) to resolve the problem. In 1883 he brought into partnership an experienced cotton spinner from Dukinfield, John Edward Lawton and it was Lawton who breathed new life into Masson Mill.

Renaissance

With new machinery, new working practices and new supervisors imported from Lancashire, Masson entered the growing market for sewing thread created by the popularity of sewing machines. A measure of Lawton's success is the substantial mansion he built, Woodbank, later, Cromford Court, overlooking Masson Mill.

By 1890, Masson Mill was exporting its products to Melbourne, Calcutta, Madras, Constantinople, France, Spain, Mexico, Vera Cruz, Mauritius, the Canary Islands, British Columbia, Chile, Monte Video, Buenos Aires and the West Indies.

In 1897, the mill became part of the English Sewing Cotton Company. It continued in use until 1992. Work then began to adapt it to new uses and, after a major repair programme had been completed, it opened in its new form in 1999.

Cromford Mill: the Colour Works years

The Cromford Mill site was less fortunate. It had no place in Lawton's plan. Towards the end of the 19th century, sections of it were used as a brewery and one of the buildings became a laundry. The Arkwright machinery at Cromford Mill was advertised for sale but there was little interest. Platts, the great textile machinery makers, acquired a water frame and other pieces to use as exhibition items to help them sell their modern equipment. Ultimately their purchases found their way to the Helmshore museum in Lancashire where they are still to be seen. Other items were donated by the Arkwright family to the Science Museum in London. Most of the Cromford machinery is thought to have been smashed. The second mill remained in a useable state and was let to William Hollins, the inventor of Viyella, a name derived from the nearby Via Gellia, whose company was using it in 1890 when it was destroyed by fire.

Early in the 20th century, the Arkwright family sold Cromford Mills and the site was divided between a colour pigment manufacturer and a laundry. It was intensively developed, every open space pressed into service for production units. The water courses were covered over and built upon and the historic buildings disfigured by lift shafts, lean-to sheds and new doorways and window openings.

In 1929 fire destroyed two floors of the first mill (Building 18), and in 1961 fire reduced the bow fronted building (the Barracks) to a shell which was subsequently demolished.

Rescue and conservation

By 1979, it was no longer economic to manufacture colour pigments at Cromford Mill. It was purchased by the Arkwright Society, the local civic society for the Matlock area. The Society embarked on an incremental strategy of repair and re-use.

Cromford Mill is now home to a range of small businesses and retail outlets which provide work for approximately 100 people. At the same time, the mills operate as a popular heritage destination, welcoming visitors from all over the world.

Building the community

Tentative steps

The first houses Richard Arkwright built, the North Street terraces of 1776-77, epitomised the essence of what was to become a pattern for the Derwent Valley factory masters. Children were perceived to be an under-utilised resource in society, and with machinery available which was simple to operate they became the workhorses of the factory system.

Once the factory masters had tied themselves to child labour delivered in family units, rather than the apprentice labour favoured by, for example, the Gregs at Styal Mill, they were inexorably committed to house building and to community development. If their mills were to flourish, the families which migrated to the new factory colonies must also flourish, and this meant providing jobs for those members of the workforce who would not find employment at the mill. Many years later a member of the Strutt family declared this to be the hardest part to deliver, and claimed his family's mills in Belper would have grown larger but for the difficulty in finding adult male employment in and around the town.

In North Street, Richard Arkwright proposed a neat solution. He would offer employment to the wives and children of the weavers who occupied the houses and in the workshops, on the topmost floor, they would weave his yarn into calico. All the Derwent Valley factory masters did much the same. Peter Nightingale could not have been more explicit when he established his own mill and advertised for labour in 1784.

"Weavers, good Calico weavers may be employed and if they have large families, may be accommodated with houses and have employment for their children".

Nightingale at Lea, in his lead works, and Evans at Darley Abbey with the paper mill, corn mill and other long established water-powered businesses close to the cotton mills, which employed predominantly adult male labour, used these connections to support their cotton mills. The Strutts employed men on their farms and as carriers and in many other capacities, but they also invested in nailshops

Weavers workshop, windows now partly blocked

and framework knitters' workshops. As early as 1790 the Strutts had built a nailshop in Belper Lane and were still investing in new nailshops in the 1830s.

The weavers Arkwright attracted to Cromford were not limited to those who found a home in North Street. There were others working in the loom shop at the mill; also at the mill there is believed to have been space set aside for framework knitters. Each of these predominantly male occupations played their part in insuring the child labour force was maintained.

The factory village takes shape

After 1789 with the Cromford estate in their own hands, the Arkwrights developed the village skilfully and energetically. The creation of the Market Place gave the settlement a new focus. Traders were attracted to the Saturday market Sir Richard established and were offered inducements to maintain their attendance. At the end of a year prizes such as beds, presses, clocks, chairs etc. were awarded to the bakers, butchers etc. who had attended the market most consistently.

> 'by 2 o'clock I was at the Black Dog at Cromford; around which is much levelling of ground, and increase of buildings for their new market, (for this place is now so popular as not to do without) which has already been once held, and will be again tomorrow'

In due course the settlement the Arkwrights had planted and nurtured became a viable economic entity. It continued to grow until c.1840. The cotton mills had by then reached their height or even started to contract as the effects of the dispute over the Cromford water supply began to be felt. It is not known how closely the Arkwrights maintained a tie

Cromford

	Houses	Population
1801	208	1115
1811	239	1259
1821	238	1242
1831	239	1291

between residence in their cottages in Cromford and work at their mills. As late as 1866 the Strutt rent books imply a close linkage, rent still being deducted from the weekly wages. No similar records survive for Cromford and with the premature decline of Cromford Mill it seems likely that by 1850 some at least of the Cromford housing would have been occupied by families who had no connection with the mills. It is also interesting to note that as early as 1816 half the Cromford Mill workforce of 725 lived outside Cromford and therefore in houses which were not linked to their employer.

Making people do their best

Even before he took possession of the Cromford estate, Arkwright had established his reputation as an employer who recognised the need for his new community to foster its own identity, social life and tradition. He is credited with the creation of customs in Cromford similar to those which existed elsewhere in older established settlements.

So, in September each year (and certainly by 1776) there was the annual festival of candle lighting when workmen and children, led by a band and a boy working in a weaver's loom, paraded from the mills round the village. On their return to the mills they received buns, ale, nuts and fruit. In 1778 on such an occasion, a song was performed "in full chorus amongst thousands of spectators from Matlock Bath and the neighbouring Towns".

As Sylas Neville observed, Arkwright "by his conduct appears to be a man of great understanding and to know the way of making his people do their best. He not only distributes pecuniary rewards but gives distinguishing dresses to the most deserving of both sexes, which excites great emulation".

> Come let us all here join in one,
> And thank him for all favours done;
> Let's thank him for all favours still
> which he hath done besides the mill.
>
> Modistly drink liquor about,
> And see whose health you can find out;
> This will I chuse before the rest
> Sir Richard Arkwright is the best.
>
> A few more words I have to say
> Success to Cromford's market day.

Verse pinned to the door of The Greyhound

The Cromford community was also sustained by the creation of various clubs and friendly societies including a cow club, but the full range and details of this provision is unknown. Information is sparse also for the educational investment in Cromford. In 1785 a Sunday School was established which immediately attracted 200 children; subsequently there was a day school, the precursor of the school erected in 1832 and which remains open.

The religious life of the community was less well provided for. The chapel built in 1777 on the edge of Matlock Bath by Arkwright's partner Samuel Need, near the spot which was later to accommodate Masson Mill, was clearly intended for Matlock Bath's fashionable visitors rather than the mill workforce. In any case, its life was cut short by Need's death in 1781; and when it did re-open in 1785 it was soon in the hands of an extreme Calvinist sect serving a small congregation. It was not until 1797, when Richard

Ye num'rous Assembly that make up this Throng,
Spare your Mirth for a Moment, and list to my Song,
The Bounties let's sing that our Master belong
At the Cotton Mills now at Cromford
The famous renown'd Cotton Mills,

Our number we count seven Hundred or more,
All cloathed and fed from his bountiful Store,
Then envy don't flout us, nor say any's poor, etc.

Ye know we all ranged in Order have been,
Such a Sight in all Europe sure never was seen,
While thousands did view us to complete the Scene, etc.

Likewise for to make our Procession more grand,
We were led in Front by a Musical band,
Who were paid from the Fund of that bountiful Hand, etc.

Ye Hungry and Naked, all hither repair,
No longer in Want don't remain in despair,
You'll meet with Employment, and each get a Share, etc.

Ye Crafts and Mechanics, if ye will draw nigh,
No longer ye need to lack an Employ,
And each duly paid, which is a great Joy, etc.

To our noble Master, a Bumper then fill,
The matchless Inventor of this Cotton Mill,
Each toss of his Glass with a hearty Good-will
With Huzza for the Mills now at Cromford
All join with a jovial Huzza

Song of 1778, sung to tune: The Roast Beef of Old England

Belper

Jedediah Strutt's first cotton mill

There was nothing tentative about Jedediah Strutt's entry into cotton spinning on his own account. Unlike Richard Arkwright, he came to the business with considerable wealth and, by waiting until Arkwright had demonstrated the full potential of his mechanical inventions and production systems, he was able to invest in a full-scale production unit without having to embark on his own expensive research and development.

It is generally assumed he began building his first mill in Belper in 1776. This is the date accepted by most authorities. However, the evidence of Strutt's land purchases puts this in doubt. It was not until 1777 that he bought the first parcels of land on which he was to build, and those 10 acres, plus small purchases made a year later, secured for him the entire site on which all the Strutt mills in Belper were to be built.

The river and the adjoining land had never before accommodated a mill at this point. There were no existing weirs or water courses and Strutt had to create his own. A weir was built across the river near the present day railway bridge and a goyt, part of which survives in the River Gardens, which linked it to the mill. It is unlikely the mill could have been ready for use in 1778 as the Strutts told the factory commission in 1834, and the advertisement for children to work in the mills in September 1781 may mark the actual completion date. A second mill was added in 1784 and it was out of the shell of this building that the fire-proof North Mill was created in 1804 after fire had destroyed the earlier structure.

Arkwright junior opened Cromford Church - which his father had planned as a private chapel for Willersley Castle - that the community's needs were catered for. The Church was in these early years pressed into service as an adjunct of factory discipline. Unlike the Strutts, the Arkwrights are not known to have encouraged other denominations to establish themselves in their village. The several Methodist sects with their own chapels, which prospered in Cromford in the 19th century were all built on land outside the Arkwright estate.

We went to church at Cromford where is a chapel built abt. 3 years and ½ ago by Mr Arkwright...On each side the Organ is a gallery in which about 50 boys were seated. These children are employed in Mr Arkwrights works in the week days, and on Sundays attend a School where they receive education. They came to Chapel in regular order and looked healthy & well & were decently cloathed and clean... The whole Plan appears to be such as to do Mr Arkwright great credit".

Joseph Farrington, diary extract, 1801

Milford

Strutt next turned his attention to Milford where, in March 1781, he bought Makeney forge and, soon after, adjoining property. Later in the same year he bought Hopping Mill Meadow, a site which included a fulling and dyeing mill. Advertisements for labour suggest the mill Strutt built here was still being constructed as late as 1784. By 1789 there were two mills at work on the site, one of which was a printing mill. In 1788, the Strutts had expressed the intention of taking up bleaching and had turned to Samuel Oldknow for advice; it is probable that it was his expertise in printing that enabled them to establish their Milford mill. A further mill was constructed in 1793.

The Belper Mill complex c.1930

William Strutt and his brothers

The development of the Belper and Milford mill sites and the Strutt mill in Derby owed much to William Strutt's engineering skills and creative talents. The clearance of the Belper and Milford sites c.1960 removed a range of mill structures which, taken together, demonstrated the evolution of William Strutt's experiments in fire-proofing mill buildings. Of his mill structures, only the North Mill at Belper remains. This remarkable building emerged in 1804 from the burned out shell of Strutt's second Belper mill. William Strutt used cast iron and brick, incorporating improvements derived from the systems Bage had used in his fire-proof structures at Shrewsbury and Leeds.

View of Strutts' Cotton Mill at Milford from a watercolour by Zachariah Boreman, 1787

In 1789 the Strutts valued their investments in the mills at Belper and Milford at £26,000 and £11,000 respectively and claimed a return of £36,000 per annum. No doubt it was this income stream and the proceeds of their hosiery business which drove forward the Strutts' development of their Belper site. The construction of the West Mill began in 1793 and was still in progress at the end of 1796. It was 61 metres long and, like the Strutts' earlier fire-proof building in Derby, it made use of brick arches and floors, hollow pot arches in the sixth storey and timber beams supported by iron columns. It was powered by two water wheels, one of 12.2 and the second of 14.6 metres width and diameters of 5.5 and 3.7 metres respectively. The goyt which had serviced the two earlier mills was no longer adequate and it was necessary to build a more substantial weir, dig out the banks of the river, and from the vast acreage of water so created, take a supply from a new cut running close by the North Mill and across the site to the new West Mill. By August 1796, the design and location of the new weir had been sketched on a plan and over the next 12 months, this remarkable structure was completed. Over the same period, the Strutts rebuilt the bridge which had been destroyed by a flood in 1795. The new bridge was completed in 1797.

William Strutt's contributions to the Derwent Valley sites continued with the Belper reeling mill in 1808; the South Mill in 1812 (a replacement of the first of the Strutt mills in Belper); and in 1813, the Round Mill, said to have been modelled on the idea of the Panopticon of Samuel and Jeremy Bentham. He also turned his hand to the improvement of mill machinery and is said to have introduced his own version of mule spinning years before it was successful elsewhere.

Unlike the Arkwrights, whose enthusiasm for the cotton industry scarcely outlived Sir Richard, the Strutts continued to innovate, invest and expand - at least while Jedediah's three sons, William (1756-1830), George Benson (1761-1841), and Joseph (1765-1844) ran the business. During the first quarter of the 19th century it remained a major force in the industry, employing by 1833 as many as 2,000 people. But the centre of the industry had moved north to Lancashire. The business was no longer well served by its location, both in relation to raw materials, the market and for access to new developments.

The Strutts also maintained a commitment to child employment long after it had become clear that with machinery growing in size and complexity the proportion of adults or at least older children employed would have to increase. The Strutts tried to swim against this tide. In Anthony Radford Strutt's words, "infant labour being so much cheaper than adult, one's attention is always directed to make such improvements in machinery as to enable children to do with ease and exactness the work of adults" (1833).

The scale of the operation gradually contracted and during the second half of the 19th century, some of the Milford site was given up and let out to other businesses.

When Edward Strutt (1801-80), William's only son, received a peerage in 1856, taking the title 'Lord Belper', the appointment was welcomed in the press as the elevation of a manufacturer, implying that Edward Strutt still earned his living as a cotton master. If he did, and certainly he was still engaged in the business, it was on a very different basis to the daily toil his father's generation had known. Day-to-day management had passed to paid staff. The Strutts, a generation later than the Arkwrights, came to enjoy a life of landed gentility.

The Strutt community in Belper

It now requires a conscious effort to distinguish the Strutt settlement from the older Belper community. Over the years the two have coalesced, but in the 1780s they would have been separated by a green no man's land nearly a quarter of a mile in width. The older settlement, based on agriculture and nailing, had been growing steadily as a market centre even before Jedediah planted his first mill nearby and it is clear that this growth continued alongside, and was further stimulated by the later Strutt investments.

Choosing a community which already had an economic infrastructure meant that the Strutts were spared some of the problems which faced Richard Arkwright in Cromford, a smaller and less developed community. Belper had a market place, public houses, shops and a chapel. From 1801 the town also had a rapidly growing hosiery business established by John Ward and others and later including George Brettle. By c.1830 the one business had become two and Belper could claim two of the largest hosiery firms in the country. The hosiers bought yarn from Strutt's, they also provided further employment in the town in the warehouses and mending rooms so helping to sustain Belper's accelerating growth.

The Strutts' land purchases in Belper and Milford followed the same pattern and priority. The first steps were associated with securing land for the mills. In Belper, almost all the purchases between 1777 and 1786 related to the mill and the

January 15th 1801	
An account of dwelling houses and sundry other buildings in the Liberty of Belper.	
Bridge Hill House and appurtenances	11
Farmhouses and appurtenances	38
Ale House and appurtenances	20
Other dwelling houses	814
Total dwelling houses	873
Cotton Mills	3
Hosiers warehouses	1
Nailers warehouses	6
Hat Factories	2
Potteries	1
Tan-Yard	1
Corn Mills	4
Malthouses	2
Bake Houses	12
Mercers, grocers, butchers shops	35
Joiners shops	7
Blacksmith's shops	7
Nailers shops	162
Stockinger's shops	27
Weaver's shops	14
	284

Nailers' workshop, Belper

acquisition of land which controlled the river. The same first steps were taken in Milford where, until 1791, land purchases were concentrated on the immediate area of the mill site and the adjoining meadow.

In Belper, it was not until 1787-88 that Strutt made the crucial purchase which would enable him to build his chapel, later to be known as the Unitarian Chapel, and the houses around it, the Short Rows. By 1801, there were 893 houses (built or being built) in Belper, an increase of 460 over the estimate made by Pilkington in 1789. Thus, in 1801, Strutt owned some 280 houses, or about a third of the total number of houses in Belper. It is clear there were others investing in Belper's growth apart from the Strutts, just as it is also clear

The Unitarian Chapel, 1788

in physical terms that Belper never became truly 'Struttsville' - the company town with total ownership of the settlement in the mill owner's hands, as was the case in Cromford and in Darley Abbey.

During the 1790s the Strutts turned their attention to building up their estate. This was made possible by the Enclosure Award of 1791 which brought with it many opportunities to purchase small parcels of land. Whereas in the first 10 years of development in Belper and Milford Jedediah had bought 48 acres of land, in the following five years, 1786-91, 144 acres were added; and between 1792 and 1796 a further 185 acres. When Jedediah Strutt died in 1797, the estate totalled around 380 acres.

There is no obvious pattern to the Strutts' house building. The earliest housing, which is thought to be the Short Rows, close to the chapel of 1788, was on the meanest scale, some, if not all, originally containing two cells, one up and one down. This was followed in 1790 by the back-to-backs in Berkin's Court; but by this time, houses of better quality, three-storey houses, were being erected at Belper Lane.

Belper	Houses	Population
1801	893	4500
1811	1043	5778
1821	1262	7235
1831	1547	7890

The growth of Belper 1801-31

During the years of 1792-97 the bulk of the three-storey houses in Long Row, Hopping Hill and Smith's Court were built. Finally, concluding the first phase of house building, the Belper cluster houses were added in 1805.

Of all the surviving examples of this house type, those in Belper most obviously demonstrate the intention to make

these houses the first choice for the most important members of the workforce, the overseers. In Belper, unlike Darley Abbey, each had an extension, a substantial garden and an individual lavatory and pigsty.

The documentary evidence which has survived suggests that the tie between working in the mill and residence in a Strutt house was strictly enforced and remained in existence as late as the 1860s. The rent books which include all known Strutt housing, demonstrate how rent was collected through deductions from the wages of the member of the household concerned. The variety of house types in the Strutt housing stock and the range of rents charged to the residents leaves no doubt there was a hierarchy. The best houses, the Clusters or Field Row, could cost 4s 6d per week while at the other end of the scale a house in the Short Rows or Mount Pleasant could be as little as 1s 3d. Smiths Court and Long Row were around 2s 6d. What is not clear is how the houses were allocated. From the tariff it seems unlikely it was arranged on the basis of family size.

A very large business

The size of the workforce in Belper and Milford has been used to suggest that Strutt's was the largest cotton factory enterprise in the United Kingdom in the early years of the 19th century, but comparisons between the competing claims of the Arkwright empire, New Lanark and the Strutts' business are difficult. What is certain is the supremacy of the Strutt business within the Derwent Valley.

In 1789, there were judged to be 800 people employed at Cromford and Masson and no more than 600 in Belper and Milford. Yet by 1802, though the Arkwright business had grown to 1,150, the Strutts now employed 1,200 to 1,300, a figure which grew steadily until a plateau was reached around 2,200 in the early 1820s. Subsequently, though there were peaks and troughs, the business maintained this level until at least the 1850s, after which consistent employment information ceases to be available. In Milford, employment reflected a different pattern. Between 1823 and 1837 the number employed in the mill fell from 537 to about 360, and there were corresponding falls among the in- workers, the skilled staff who maintained the machinery. But in March 1824 the foundry and the gas works opened, a year later a dye works; by 1837 this employed over 70 people.

The hours worked in the mills were six before dinner, which was taken between 12 and 1, and six after dinner with time allowed within each six hour period for breakfast and tea. The Strutts were quite clear that the basic day had been inherited from the Derby Silk Mill where "this has been the

Being off drinking
Off at Derby Races without leave
Stealing packthread
Stealing yarn the property of Messrs. Srutts'
Breaking a Drawing Frame
Breaking a pair of scales
Stopping four frames at once
Leaving her machine dirty
Counting hanks wrong
Idleness and looking throu' windows
Calling through some window to some soldiers
Making noises in Counting House
Making T Ride's nose bleed on the hanks
For putting Josh Haynes' dog in a bucket of Hot water
Rubbing their faces with blood and going about the town to frighten people
Terrifying S Pearson with her ugly face

Belper Mill forfeits 1805-1813

Moscow Farm

invariable practice... for more than 100 years". Discipline within the works was maintained by overseers and by a system of fines. Outside working hours, watchmen employed by the Strutts' reported anyone whose behaviour became too wayward. In the early days payment was largely in truck and no more than one sixth was in cash. Deductions were made from wages for rent, food stuffs, coal, milk and vegetables. Some of the produce came from part of the Strutt estate, the garden of Bridge Hill House and from Wyver Farm.

Feeding the community

The milk supply was a matter of special concern. The Strutts established a dairy and to see that it received milk throughout the year, they agreed to buy such quantities of milk from suppliers at a price that made it worthwhile keeping cows through the winter, the suppliers paying the Strutts if the supply fell short. Here again, some of the supply was from the Strutts' own farms at Bridge Hill and Green Hall. The provision of tea and coffee, which began in 1826, attracted attention because of the arrangement whereby any profits were used to pay for medical care required by any of the subscribers. There was also a sick club for all females employed in the mills, which may have been set up as early as 1801 and was certainly in existence by 1821.

By 1821 the Strutts had established the Belper Provision Company, a co-operative enterprise which distributed profits among its customers in proportion to the value of their purchases. A similar society existed in Milford. The arrangements to sell milk continued until April 1854, by which time the scheme had been running for some years at a

modest loss. It is not clear whether it was cost or lack of demand which led the Strutts to dismantle this well intentioned strategy.

The Strutts demonstrated their belief in toleration by assisting others to provide places of worship in Belper and Milford. Jedediah's personal convictions led him to build a chapel in Belper and provide accommodation in Milford for those who shared his Unitarian faith, and the company continued to support the Belper Unitarian chapel financially until at least 1847. But the Strutts were not doctrinaire in their beliefs and actively encouraged other denominations to establish places of worship sometimes contributing financially or by making a gift of land.

Education and music

The Strutts' commitment to education embraced Sunday Schools and Day Schools and a number of cultural initiatives which seem far ahead of their time. Before the introduction of the half-time system, the Strutts insisted upon children attending day school before they were offered work in the mills, so guaranteeing a certain level of literacy among their labour force. By 1817, 64 children were attending Day Schools and 650 the Sunday Schools at Belper, while at Milford 300 were in the Lancasterian Sunday School and the numbers grew as the company and facilities expanded. The Strutts insisted on attendance at Sunday School for all their young employees under 20. The cultural life of the community was also taken care of with dancing and meeting rooms made available at the mills and through John Strutt's band. This was in fact a 40 strong orchestra and choir recruited from work people employed at the mills. They received regular instruction in work time and in return agreed to remain in the Strutts' employment for at least seven years. The orchestra performed in and around Derby. John Strutt rewarded the members of his orchestra with occasional visits to the opera and to concerts in London.

> On Monday, the female hands in their employ, to the number of nearly 1,000, were entertained by Jedediah Strutt Esq., on the lawn in front of his beautiful residence, by a sumptuous dejeuner, the excellent band of John Strutt Esq. playing the most approved airs.
>
> In the evening they adjourned in procession to the large area of the mills when the day was delightfully concluded by a merry trip on the "light fantastic toe", in one of the large and appropriate rooms of those immense edifices.
>
> During these gratifying festivities 4,800 lbs of beef, 3,184 lbs of plum pudding, 7,000 penny loaves and 2,500 quarts of ale were distributed".

Derby Mecury report, 1832

Like the Arkwrights at Cromford the Strutts were not slow to recognise the value of communal celebrations in fostering social cohesion and loyalty. The events which thrilled Belper and Milford were generally in honour of some great national news. In 1802 it was the treaty of Amiens; in 1814 the declaration of peace; in 1821 the coronation of George IV ; but it was the passage of the Reform Bill which produced the most whole-hearted reaction. "The festivities in honour of the reform bill", the Derby Mercury reported, "have been conducted at Belper on a scale, that we doubt not will equal if not surpass any other in the country. The whole has been arranged by a Committee of Management, aided by the invincible energy of their justly popular towns men, Messrs Strutt".

Darley Abbey

Amassing the land to build the cotton mills

The association of the Evans' name with Darley Abbey started long before 1782 but the impression is misleading. There were in fact two families bearing the name Evans which were unrelated to one another until 1751 when Thomas Evans, 1723-1814, married Sarah Evans, the daughter of Alderman William Evans of Derby.

Alderman Evans had held industrial interests in Darley Abbey since at least 1746 when he acquired a fulling mill and dye house, but it was not until the 1770s that Thomas Evans and his brother the Reverend Edmund Evans began the purchase of the land holding which was to form the Evans industrial estate. In 1773 Edmund paid Abraham Hirst of Derby £1010-10s-0d for a corn mill, a paper mill, a flint mill and a china mill together with other buildings used by the paper mill; and this together with further purchases made by Thomas Evans in 1774 and 1775, secured for the two brothers all the industrial premises then extant in Darley Abbey.

But the estate the brothers had bought did not include land outside the long established industrial settlement. This lay to the south of the rocky out crop where later the weir was constructed at the point where the river turns in a wide sweep to the south east. The land to the north, where the cotton mills were to be built, was not acquired until 1778. It was an expensive purchase costing £1,140 for 7.1 hectares of land. The substantial cost surely reflects the potential for water-powered industrial use, which both parties in this transaction recognised and Thomas, his son William and Thomas's brother Edmund began.

Belper transport links

Before the Cromford and Derby canals were built, raw cotton was brought from Gainsborough along the Trent and Derwent rivers to Derby and by road to Milford and Belper. No satisfactory road ran through the Derwent Valley flood plain until 1817. The turnpike road from Derby to Chesterfield built in 1739, followed the high ground on the west side of the river from Derby to Milford. From there, having crossed the river by a ford, it continued to Chesterfield across the higher ground to the east.

Jedediah Strutt and Thomas Evans petitioned against the Cromford Canal Bill of 1789, as they feared water supply to it would threaten the water power for their mills. The Canal was completed in 1794, and although a branch was proposed in 1801, from near Ambergate to Belper, it was not built. A network of tramways, including one owned by the Strutts, enlarged the catchment areas of the Cromford and Derby canals particularly for coal and limestone. The tramway from the Derby Canal at Little Eaton to Denby was extended to the east side of Belper, to supply coal to the town. Until 1817, when economic success justified the building of a turnpike in the valley to Cromford (now the A6), Belper was linked by way of the Chesterfield turnpike to the Cromford Canal at Heage. Later the wharf at Ambergate was used, although increasingly, until the opening of the railway in 1840, Derby became the main distribution point for raw cotton for Milford and Belper.

Derwent Valley Mills Nominated
World Heritage Site ▬

Canal ▬

Proposed Canal 1801 ▪▪▪▪

Former Turnpike Road(s) A6 ▬

River Derwent ﹏

Railway Line ▪▪▪▪

Turnpike ▬

Tramway ▬

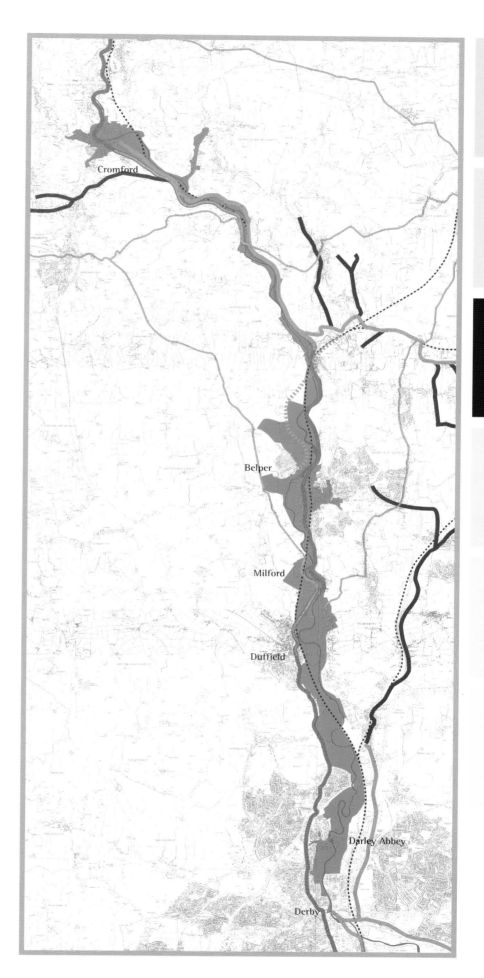

A partnership with Richard Arkwright

It has to be assumed that this enterprise was planned with the full co-operation of Richard Arkwright, with whom the Evans already worked closely. Indeed, in the early days of the project, it would appear Richard Arkwright and the Evans family were partners. The evidence is contained in the insurance policy Richard Arkwright purchased late in 1782 from the Sun Insurance Company with "William and Edmund Evans for their water cotton mill". The mill was described as "stone and tiled" and the policy valued it at £800.

The first Darley Abbey cotton mill

Little is known of the first Evans mill. A plan drawn by Benjamin Outram in 1792 indicates that the first leat bringing water to the mill was located to the east of the building. In 1788 the mill was damaged severely by fire and much of it had to be rebuilt. Its replacement, known as Long Mill, the earliest of the buildings in the surviving mill complex, contains substantial elements of the earlier building.

In its first incarnation the mill had a very limited life. There is evidence which suggests it was not ready for production until late in 1786 when Richard Arkwright agreed to lease it from Thomas Evans. The suggestion that the first mill was not ready for production until about this time is further supported by the following advertisement in the Derby Mercury in 1787.

> "Darley Abbey cotton mill. WANTED. Families Particularly women and children to work at Said Mill. They may be provided with comfortable houses and every convenience at Darley or Allestry: particularly a milking cow to each family. It is a very good neighbourhood for the men getting work who are not employed in the manufactory".

The lease with Richard Arkwright was never completed and in 1787 Evans was still buying components from gear cutters and clock makers in Ashbourne and from iron founders to equip the mill with machinery, further evidence of the time it took to fully commission a mill of this size. At the same time he was attempting to find a market for his first production of yarn.

The mill rebuilt and extended

After barely a year the Evans Mill was destroyed by fire. Rebuilding began immediately. The mill had been insured so the Evans escaped total loss. No further set-backs are recorded.

It is known that the mill was extended to the east between 1796 and 1805 with a new cut and new buildings and map evidence of 1811 reveals that by this date a West Mill had been built. Further extensions were made between 1818 and 1821. The enterprise also expanded to the north of the original mill site where a number of new processes were installed and ancillary functions such as the counting house and offices and stabling were housed.

The mills now employed more than 500 people and growth continued until c.1830. In the later years of the 19th century the business retained and developed further the integration and self sufficiency which in the earliest years had been a necessity. Though ultimately spinning was given up and mule-spun yarn was imported from Lancashire, the company continued all the other manufacturing processes including dyeing and added the manufacture of the bobbins on which the thread was sold and by 1862, the printing of labels and promotional material.

A mature and successful enterprise

A catalogue for the 'Boar's Head Cotton Manufactory, Derby' has survived from September 26, 1855, which lists all Walter Evans & Co's products. It includes Sewing, Tambour (embroidery), Mending, Knitting Cotton and Haberdashery, and it is clear that in addition to Evans' own output, goods were being bought in for resale. In this way the Evans' service to their retailers could be made more comprehensive. Such items included sarsnet, a fine soft silk material used for lining dresses; ferrets, a tape of cotton or silk; galloons, ribbons of gold or silver thread used to trim garments; and handkerchiefs, braces, pins, needles, bonnet wire, buttons and whalebone.

The Evans' seem to have been first among the Derwent Valley factory masters to develop a retail as well as an industrial or commercial presence and attempt to serve the market which existed in people's homes for sewing cottons, knitting cottons and embroidery threads and materials.

3. History and Development - Darley Abbey

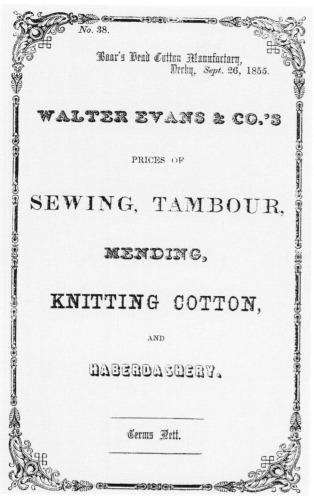

Sales catalogue, 1855

Evans had agents in London, Manchester, Blackburn, Leicester and Nottingham and travellers who covered other centres such as Birmingham.

Their brand name, Boar's Head, a name suggested by the family coat of arms which included a boar's head, was in use by the middle of the century. Boar's Head thread was exported all over the world except to those markets where a porcine image might be culturally offensive. In these cases alternative brand names were used.

Box and bobbin labels. From the 1840's Walter Evans & Co were prepared to package their products with the names of retail outlets. In this example Mrs B. Lomax of Cases Street, Liverpool.

In 1862 a visitor noted that Boar's Head crochet cotton was still being wound by hand and that much of this work was carried out "by the people of Darley in their own homes". It is likely that this was the last of the outwork. When the mills first opened it would have been extensive. Cotton picking, still at this time an unmechanised process, was dealt with outside the mill and some of it was put into the hands of contractors. As the firm acquired batting and willow machines the demand for pickers grew less. James Huthwaite discovered this in October 1803 when (Evans)

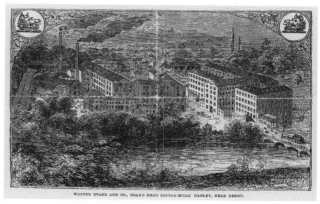

Boar's Head Mill 1862

"gave him notice that it was uncertain how long his hands could be employed to pick for Walter Evans & Co and that he must give the worst of his hands a month's notice on his return home".

In the 1860s and '70s, Boar's Head products won international recognition: at the London exhibitions of 1861 and 1862; in Dublin in 1865; in Paris in 1867; in Vienna in 1873 and in Paris in 1879.

The end of the line

The Evans' involvement in the business ceased with the death of Walter Evans in 1903. John Peacock, who had been manager, bought the mills from his estate. The Peacocks ran the business until 1943, when it was taken over by J & P Coats. In 1969 the sale of the mills for other uses began. The mills are now home to a variety of small businesses.

Darley Abbey: housing and the development of the community

Darley Abbey contains examples of the classic Derwent Valley three-storey mill workers' terraces similar to the earliest Cromford housing; but it also has a significant number of back-to-back houses, a house type not found in Cromford though present in Belper and Milford, and it has the earliest known example of the cluster house.

This design was promoted by Charles Bage as housing suitable for overseers at the Flax Mill he designed in 1797 for Marshalls on the outskirts of Shrewsbury. It was also used by William Strutt in Belper where, while there is no evidence that the cluster houses were reserved for overseers, it is clear from the rent that they were considered the best the Strutts had to offer their workers. In Darley Abbey it is by no means certain that Four Houses was intended to provide superior accommodation. The houses were no larger than many others in Darley Abbey and there is no evidence of the extensive gardens, private privies and pigsties which made the Belper cluster houses so attractive to those who could afford to live in them.

The cluster blocks in New Road on the other hand may once have come closer to providing superior accommodation than appearances now suggest. But even here it is difficult to see how the curtilage could have contained adequate space for gardens, privies and sties on the scale offered in Belper. However, the two blocks in Lower New Road, in their original form, may have been of a higher quality.

It is tempting to see the hands of Charles Bage and William Strutt at work in Darley Abbey and with William Strutt's family connection with the Evans' and Charles Bage's family links with Darley Abbey this is a point worthy of serious consideration. There is however no documentary evidence to substantiate such a claim.

The growth of the community

The growth of the community followed the development of the mills. Between 1788 and 1801 the settlement doubled. Growth was a more measured 22% in the next decade followed by minimal growth, 7%, between 1811 and 1821. But the substantial investment in mill building and machinery in the years 1818-21 was followed in turn by a 37% increase in housing stock by 1831; after which, for the rest of the century, growth was minimal.

Darley Abbey		
	Houses	Population
1801	95	615
1811	116	796
1821	125	841
1831	172	1170

The growth of Darley Abbey, 1801-31

Much of the evidence of the Evans' concern to nurture their mill community is in the mill ledgers rather than in bricks and mortar. There is of course the church built in 1819 and

the school which was constructed in 1826, but their record of educational provision had begun at least 30 years earlier. In 1791, a Sunday School was planned for the attic floor of the

mill, and five years later 80 children employed at the mill were attending the Evans' Sunday School. A day school, teaching children to read and knit, at a cost of one penny and a farthing per week, was in existence by 1797; and two years later there was a night school. Health care was also provided both to residents who were ill and in the form of mass inoculation against smallpox: 79 children in 1797 and 88 in 1800. There was also a club which was organised on the same lines as a Friendly Society, to which members contributed and which paid a weekly sum to members who were unable to work.

Feeding the community was also a major concern for the Evans. Unlike Cromford, Darley Abbey had no market place or public houses, nor is it clear in the early years of this cotton mill community that there were shops. Essential products were however purchased by the mill owners and sold to the residents at cost or at a slight loss. Milk was bought from the tenants of the Evans' farms in Allestree and Darley Abbey and sold at tuppence ha'penny a quart. Flour, oatmeal, cheese, beer, coal and blankets were sold on a similar basis though it is not clear that such products were always available or whether they were provided only in times of hardship.

Survival and change

Over the last 40 years new building has obliterated many of Darley Abbey's green spaces and it requires an act of the imagination to recapture an impression of its pastoral character and of the self-sufficiency of its residents. So much of the allotment and grazing land has gone; the cottages now stand in a suburban rather than a rural setting. But the mill ledgers prove that the cows promised to prospective residents in the newspaper advertisements were a reality. Somewhere space was found for them and for the gardens and allotments. And there can be no doubting the importance of the garden and the allotments in sustaining the community.

In 1930, following the death of Ada Evans, the widow of Walter Evans', the estate was sold. Subsequently the two Evans' houses, Darley House which had been built by William Evans in the 1780s and where Elizabeth his widow received Samuel Taylor Coleridge in 1796 (Coleridge described her as "without exception the greatest woman I have been fortunate enough to meet with in my brief pilgrimage through life"), and Darley Hall- purchased by Samuel Evans in 1835 - have both been demolished. It is now more than 70 years since a member of the Evans dynasty exercised influence and control over the lives of residents in Darley Abbey, yet some evidence of an autocratic past remains to this day.

Linking Darley Abbey to the outside world

Thomas Evans was as entrepreneurial in improving his factory community's transport links as he was in his other business decisions. In 1792 he instigated a plan to link the river Derwent to the Derby Canal and to make it navigable to Darley Abbey weir. Benjamin Outram was commissioned to survey and prepare proposals and a plan has survived which sets out Outram's route for a towpath up the east bank of the river to Darley Abbey where a wharf was to be built. For a while the mill had its own boat. In May 1788 it sank and had to be salvaged and repaired. No evidence to confirm the precise location of the Darley Abbey Wharf has been found. The Derby Canal link provided Darley Abbey with direct access to the canal system and to the river Trent which, with Gainsborough as the principal port, remained a major artery for goods coming into this part of the region until the coming of the railways.

Of special importance for Evans was the Grand Trunk (or Trent-Mersey) Canal which he used to export his products to the key market in Manchester which he attempted to supply on a weekly basis.

In 1798-99 the Evans' improved the community's road links by upgrading Mile Ash Lane up the hill to join the Derby turnpike. Before and after the improved road had been built the Mile Ash tollhouse was used as a collection point for goods. So in September 1793, when Evans was expecting ironwork from the Alderwasley forge, he wrote "Mr Geo Strutt writes us he has ordered you to send a wheel and pinion from his model to be laid down at the turnpike". Waggoners were a constant problem. In June 1799, the iron pillars for the cotton mill which were on their way from Smiths in Chesterfield turned out to have been "left at Derby", the waggoner saying he did not know "they were to come hither".

Darley Abbey did not have its own rail link although the North Midland line passed close by. The nearest railhead for the Mill was via Haslam's Lane and Chester Green, Derby.

Biographical Notes

Richard Arkwright 1732-92

Sir Richard Arkwright by Joseph Wright of Derby

Richard Arkwright was born in Preston the son of Thomas Arkwright, a tailor. He received little formal education and his parents apprenticed him to a barber. He then moved to Bolton where he worked for a peruke maker, later setting up on his own. In 1755 he married his first wife, Patience Holt, and at the end of that year their son Richard was born. By the early 1760s Richard Arkwright was running a barber's shop, a public house and making wigs, for which purpose he travelled the country to buy women's hair. It was during this period he began to experiment with machinery to spin cotton. About 1764 or 1765, he met Thomas Highs and John Kay and, over the next three years, struggling against poverty - he had given up all employment to spend time on his experiments - he finally completed his work while living in the schoolmaster's house in Preston. In the spring of 1768 Richard Arkwright left Preston for Nottingham, seeking backers who would finance a patent and further develop his machine. Ultimately he was successful both with his patent and in securing men of substance in the form of Samuel Need and Jedediah Strutt to fund his mills in Nottingham and Cromford. By 1775, Arkwright's contribution to technological development was complete and the systems he devised to mechanise the pre-spinning preparatory processes were embodied in his second patent of 1775.

At the trial where Arkwright's patent was finally set aside in 1785, much was made of his dependence on others or, more bluntly, his theft of the machine he claimed to have invented. Doubts about Richard Arkwright's integrity as an inventor have persisted. Even in 1932 when Richard Arkwright's bicentenary was being celebrated, the Manchester Guardian, in a long adulatory piece, could find no way round confessing the man was probably a thief. More recently, research by Dr Richard Hills has exposed the weakness in this interpretation: the machines Arkwright is alleged to have copied contained fundamental flaws and could never have been made to work. Thus Arkwright's reputation as an inventor has been restored to him.

To Arkwright the inventor must be added Arkwright the production manager. When contemporaries wrote of the Arkwright System it was not simply a set of machines they had in mind. The Arkwright System integrated the machinery and the workforce around a common source of motive power.

After the second patent and the second Cromford Mill, Arkwright's empire grew, both by building mills which were run by his extended family or by managers who had learned their trade at Cromford and by licensed use of the machinery. Arkwright became immensely rich and began to enjoy his wealth. In 1786 he received a knighthood and in the same year began to build a mansion in Cromford, Willersley Castle. In 1788 while the Castle was being built Arkwright bought himself a town house, 8 Adam Street. He also had his portrait painted by Joseph Wright of Derby and by an American artist, Mather Brown. But if he acquired the trappings of gentility he never felt the need to live the life of a country gentleman. It is said that even "when considerably more than 50 years of age - feeling that the defects of his education placed him under great difficulty and inconvenience in conducting his correspondence, and in the general management of his business - he encroached upon his sleep, in order to gain an hour each day to learn English grammar and another hour to improve his writing and orthography".

Wedgwood also presents a picture of a man driven by his business affairs.

> *"I have visited Mr Arkwright several times and find him much more conversible than I expected, and he invites me to come and see as often as I can, though he tells me he at present shuns all company as much as possible because it robs him of his time and breaks in upon his plans - and besides he says he is no company for them, for whilst they are talking to him upon one subject he is thinking upon another, and does not know what they say to him".*

Sir Richard was reported by the Gentleman's Magazine as having "*died immensely rich, and [as having] left manufactories the income of which is greater than that of most German principalities... his real and personal property is estimated at little short of half a million*".

In an obituary in the Derby Mercury Erasmus Darwin adopted a wider perspective. Arkwright's system of spinning

> *"by giving perpetual employment to many thousand families has increased the population, and been productive of greater commercial advantages to this country, and contributed more to the general benefit of mankind, in so short a period of time, than any other single effort of human ingenuity".*

Richard Arkwright junior 1755 - 1843

Sir Richard's only son, Richard, had shared in the development of his father's cotton spinning empire learning his trade at Cromford and running mills at Rocester, Bakewell, Cressbrook and Manchester, either for his own benefit or as part of his father's business. Like his father, from the late 1780s, he had no further appetite for the cotton trade and showing shrewd judgement he sold both his own and the businesses he inherited from his father as soon

Richard Arkwright Junior and family by Joseph Wright of Derby

as it was practicable, retaining only the Masson and Cromford Mills.

His interests lay in banking, investment in government funds and in the accumulation of land. His banking concern, the Arkwright Toplis Bank, in which he became a partner in 1804 and which in 1829, three years after the death of John Toplis, became Richard Arkwright and Company, had banks in Wirksworth and Ashbourne. It was a small concern but profitable, serving the local gentry, local industry and public bodies such as enclosure commissioners. Richard Arkwright's purchase of government stocks which began in 1787 continued until towards the end of his life when he was the largest holder of Funds in England. His interests in land were fuelled partly by investment opportunity to increase his rent income but mainly by the desire to settle each of his six sons in a house and estate of befitting style. Richard also lent money to the nobility, his most celebrated client being Georgiana Duchess of Devonshire.

Richard Arkwright lived quietly at Willersley completing the Castle and Church, beautifying the grounds, creating a garden and growing grapes in his hothouse. He was not a man who engaged himself in public life though he served as a J.P. and, like his father, was High Sheriff. His support for the Tory cause was never in doubt.

He died in 1843 worth £3¼ million, a wealthier man by far than his father. Sir Richard Arkwright is remembered for his inventions - as father of the factory system - Richard Arkwright junior's achievement was the foundation of a dynasty. Such was his wealth and his insistence that it be shared amongst his children, that generation after generation of the family was able to live the comfortable life of the country gentleman.

Charles Woolley Bage c.1752-1822

Charles Woolley Bage, the noted pioneer of fire-proof mill structures, originated from Darley Abbey where his family had been involved in paper manufacture for two, or perhaps three, generations. His father Robert, 1728-1801, followed his own father George into papermaking at Darley Abbey later moving to Elford, Staffordshire where he established a papermaking business. He was famous amongst his contemporaries as an exponent of the English novel and his reputation was not confined to Britain; several of his works were translated into German. He was also part of the Midland's intellectual network which included Erasmus Darwin and the other members of the Lunar Society. In 1764 Bage and Erasmus Darwin became partners in the Wychnor ironworks which, when it was sold in 1781, left Bage in serious debt. It was this experience, he claimed, which drove him to write light novels.

Charles retained his early connections with Darley Abbey and Derby. His career took him to Shrewsbury as a wine merchant and there he fell in with a group of men of unusual ability which included Samuel Butler the Headmaster of Shrewsbury School and Thomas Telford the engineer. However, he did not lose contact with his Derbyshire friends and William Strutt was closely associated with his work on revolutionary iron building techniques, heating designs and the construction of fire-proof mills. The supreme monument to Bage's talent is the Shrewsbury Mill known as Bage's Flax Mill built in 1796-7 for John Marshall, and Thomas and Benjamin Benyan. The houses adjacent to the mill which made use of the cluster design were explicitly designed for overseers. It is difficult to escape the conclusion that their antecedents, like Bage's own, are to be found in Darley Abbey.

The Evans dynasty

Of the three Derwent Valley factory masters considered here, none entered cotton spinning from a position of greater wealth than Thomas Evans, 1723-1814. He and his brothers Edmund, 1712-91, and George, 1726-1808, grew up in a Bonsall family heavily involved in the lead industry, a foundation on which Thomas and George were to build. Thomas, when he married Sarah Evans (no relation) in 1751, daughter of William Evans, Alderman and later Mayor of Derby, was already in business in Derby as an ironmonger. Subsequently his other interests included lead smelting and merchanting at Bonsall and Wirksworth with his brother George, copper smelting at Borrowash with his father-in-law and Walter Mather, and an iron works in Derby. He became an influential banker with a counting house in St Mary's Gate, Derby. The Evans' bank, later Crompton and Evans, eventually became part of the Westminster, now NatWest Group. Other business interests included cheese factoring. Much of Thomas's wealth was invested in land in Derbyshire and Staffordshire; but he continued to live in Derby, eschewing the country house he could so well have afforded.

In 1779 Thomas Evans and his business partner Walter Mather acted for the creditors in the spectacular bankruptcy of the Derby bankers, John and Christopher Heath who left debts of over £90,000. In this transaction Evans and Mather disposed of the Heath property at Darley Abbey including Darley Hall and park, property adjoining Thomas's own land. It was not until 1835 that William and Samuel Evans were able to purchase it from the Holdens and add it to the Evans' estate. Thomas died in 1814 at the advanced age of 91 with an estate valued at over £229,000.

It was Thomas's son William who played a major part in developing the family's cotton mill interests in Darley Abbey. William established his home here, living at Darley House. He also forged an important dynastic link with the Strutt family when, in 1785 he married Jedediah's daughter Elizabeth, 1758-1836. It was Elizabeth, as a widow in 1796, who was anxious to engage the poet Samuel Taylor Coleridge as tutor to her children, a position he was ready to accept. But opposition from the Evans' family led to the abandonment of this plan. Two years later, in 1798, Elizabeth married her late husband's half brother Walter Evans, 1764-1839. It was during Walter's period in charge of the Darley Abbey enterprise that the massive expansion of the mills between 1818 and 1821 took, place bringing with it a substantial increase in the size of the community. In 1818 Walter financed and endowed St

Matthew's Church and subsequently the school. Walter's sister Barbara had, in 1793, married William Strutt, Jedediah's eldest son, thus forming a double alliance between the Evans and the Strutts.

In 1839 when Walter died his interests in Darley Abbey were mainly inherited by his two nephews William and Samuel, whom he had earlier brought into the business. Samuel, who lived in Darley Hall, took over the running of both the paper and the cotton mill businesses. William, increasingly led the life of a landed gentleman, moving to nearby Allestree Hall. When Samuel died in 1874 responsibility for running the business fell on the shoulders of his eldest son Walter, 1826-1903. Towards the end of his life Walter, while he retained ownership, passed on the day-to-day management to others, and ultimately to John Peacock who, on Walter's death in 1903, purchased the mills.

Walter Evans widow, Ada, continued to live in Darley Abbey and retained ownership of the estate. She died in 1929 and two years later the estate was sold. Substantial parts of it came into the hands of Derby Borough Council who in 1962 demolished the Hall.

Peter Nightingale 1736-1803

The founder of Lea cotton spinning mill came from a local family who, during the 18th century, had moved up the social ladder from being peasant farmers to prosperous lead smelting merchants and land owners. Peter Nightingale developed his family's lead and land interests and engaged in other industrial and commercial enterprises. He was among the promoters of the Cromford Canal Company and the Lea Bridge arm of the canal, which he built at his own expense and which linked his smelting and cotton mills to the canal network. By 1776 he had become Richard Arkwright's financial partner and landlord at Cromford. His venture into cotton spinning in 1783 was not conspicuously successful and he would have sold his mill if he had found a buyer. Arkwright took legal action against him for entering into a partnership with Benjamin Pearson, one of Arkwright's most trusted managers and for the unauthorised use of his machinery. Peter Nightingale never married but he too was linked to the Derwent Valley factory masters' network by family ties. His sister Anne married George Evans, 1726-1808, the brother of Thomas Evans, who was the banker and founder of the Darley Abbey enterprise.

For more than a century after Peter Nightingale's death his descendants continued to live in the area. Today the name Nightingale is remembered less for the achievements of Peter Nightingale the founder of the family's fortune than for the

Walter Evans & Co box and bobbins labels printed for their New York agents

Jedediah Strutt by Joseph Wright of Derby

At Derby the product was principally silk hose. The raw silk was bought in London, prepared at Strutt's Silk Mill in Derby and put out to be knitted, or knitted on the firm's own frames. It was a successful business which continued in the family's hands until 1803 and it was the profit earned in Derby which enabled Jedediah to build up his cotton spinning concerns in Belper and Milford. Jedediah's introduction to this fledgling industry arose through Richard Arkwright's search for financial support to develop the machinery he had patented in 1769 but which his original partners were unable to fund adequately. The link was Samuel Need, a wealthy Nottingham hosier and business partner of Strutt's.

He is alleged to have sent Richard Arkwright to see Jedediah Strutt in Derby and a deal was struck. Need and Strutt, on payment of £500, joined the Arkwright partnership; with their backing, Arkwright was able to start converting the premises he had leased in Nottingham, where he intended to drive his new machine by horse power. Even before production began in Nottingham, the partners had signed the Cromford lease, a step which was to have far-reaching consequences for the development of the factory system. The Cromford Mill partnership was profitable financially and, more importantly, it produced a model which could be used elsewhere.

reputation of his great niece, Florence, 1820-1910, the pioneer of hospital and nursing reform.

Jedediah Strutt 1726–97

Jedediah Strutt, 1726-97, was the son of a prosperous farmer and maltster. He was born in South Normanton and moved to Findern near Derby, when he became apprenticed to a wheelwright. The details of his early adult years are unknown, but about 1754 he returned to the area of his birth having inherited a farm from an uncle. There is more than one version of the story of his introduction to the hosiery business and of his subsequent invention, the Derby rib machine, patented in 1759. Through a series of partnerships and much aided by the nonconformist network of which he was a staunch member, the new business prospered and by 1762 Strutt was in Derby working with his brother William and other partners. His patent survived a challenge in the courts in 1766, after which his business grew substantially.

Jedediah Strutt's business was a family affair. His wife, his brother and his brother-in-law all played a part and in 1770, when he reached the age of 14, his eldest son William joined the firm. So too did the younger sons George Benson Strutt and Joseph when they left school, and from time to time their sister Elizabeth helped out.

It is known that Jedediah Strutt had a house in Cromford and is also said to have lived in Belper while the mills were being built; but his real home was Derby. Soon after building his fine house at Milford he moved to an historic mansion, Exeter House where the Young Pretender had stayed in 1745; it was here that he died in May 1797.

In his last years, relations with other members of the family had become strained, possibly as a result of his second

"Here rests in Peace J S - who, without Fortune, Family or friends raised to himself a fortune, family and Name in the World - Without having wit had a good share of plain Common Sense - Without much genius enjoyed the more substantial blessing of a sound understanding - With but little personal pride despised a mean or base Action - With no Ostentation for Religious Tenets and Ceremonies he led a life of honesty and Virtue - and nor knowing what would befall him after death, he died resigned in full Confidence that if there be a future State of retribution it will be to reward the Virtuous and the good".

Jedediah, who was prone to long peroiods of introspection, left this epitaph amongst his correspondence.

William Strutt by Ramsay Reinagle

Erasmus Darwin by Joseph Wright of Derby

marriage, and it is clear that much of the burden of running the business had been handed over to his sons.

William Strutt 1756-1830

The three brothers divided their responsibilities in the business between them. George, who lived at Bridge Hill House, a mansion overlooking the river and most of Belper, managed the mills and the estate, while from their homes in Derby, William and Joseph took charge of the technical and commercial functions.

William, despite his limited formal education, came to be regarded as an expert in the design of fire-proof buildings, in hot-air heating systems and, following the completion of his tour de force, the Derby Infirmary, in the design of hospitals.

He also corresponded with scholars on mathematical, theoretical and practical problems. Among these was Charles Bage, whom it is likely William Strutt had known from an early age. William and his brother Joseph were well regarded by some of the outstanding literary figures of their time. Coleridge and Southey both visited them.

Erasmus Darwin's friendship with William had begun in 1781. It was through Erasmus Darwin that William Strutt had access to a wider circle, which included members of the Lunar Society such as Matthew Boulton, James Watt, William Small, Joseph Priestley and Josiah Wedgwood. At a somewhat lower level of intellectual and scientific

achievement, the Derby Philosophical Society fulfilled a similar function. It had been founded by Darwin and Strutt with Erasmus acting as the first president, a role which subsequently fell to William.

William Strutt's circle also included the Benthams and Robert Owen, who wrote of William Strutt and his brother Joseph as being among "men of great practical knowledge who were much interested in my views and practical measures... two men whose talents in various ways and whose truly benevolent dispositions have seldom been equalled".

In public life William Strutt strove to improve the social and physical amenities of his home town. He took an active part in measures to improve lighting and paving and to promote the development of the gas company. He designed several of Derby's bridges. He promoted Friendly Societies and the Savings Banks.

In his design for the Derby Infirmary he displayed the whole range of his architectural and engineering genius and it became a showplace visited by medical authorities from all over the country and abroad.

William and his brothers were known for their liberal views, support of toleration and humanitarian causes including opposition to slavery.

William died a respected and much loved figure in 1830, leaving to his son Edward the 1200 acre estate at Kingston on Soar which he had purchased in 1796 using the fortune brought to the marriage by his wife Barbara, née Evans.

4 Bibliography

4   Bibliography

4 (a) Select Bibliography

Editorial Note

Any serious account of the history of the Derwent Valley factory settlements must draw heavily on the work of R S Fitton, S D Chapman and A P Wadsworth. For Milford and Darley Abbey thanks must be given to Heather Eaton, Bernard Holden and Dennis Rodwell for access to their unpublished research studies, to David Hool for his unpublished genealogical and local history material, to John Hume for commenting on the text and to Ellen Wheeldon, Doreen Buxton, George Jones, Cyril Maskery, Barry Joyce and Angus Watson for their assistance. The select bibliography which follows has been confined in its scope to manuscript sources and printed material which illuminate the history and conservation of the nominated World Heritage Site. It does not include the wider ranging literature or works of fiction.

Christopher Charlton

1. Manuscript Sources

British Library

   Additional Manuscripts: Woolley Mss. 6666-6718

Derbyshire Record Office

(a) Quarter Sessions

   Papers D Q/RP 1 and 2. Maps and Plans of roads, canals and railways (various).

   Enclosure Acts, Awards and Plans. Q/AR/ 10,48,49,56,57 and 91: Q/R 1/115. Q/Ric 11/1-3, 46/1-2 and 107

   Land Tax Returns 1780-1830 (Appletree, Morleston and Litchurch and Wirksworth Hundreds) D. Q/RE

(b)Other Collections

   Arkwright of Wirksworth, D198

   Cromford Brewery Accounts, D2211

   Cromford Canal Navigation permits, D501, 1041,1265,1366, 1391, 1534 and 2653

   Enclosure Acts, Awards and Plans, D44Z/B1: D1564: D1437/5/1/1: D2152/6/1

   Nightingale of Lea D1575, D 3585

   Sir Richard Arkwright and Co Cromford and Belper D3638

   Strutt Papers D3772. D1564

   Taylor, Simpson and Mosley Papers (Evans of Darley Abbey) D185 and D 769

   Tithe Awards and Maps, D2360/3/28,52,75,98,136 and 144. D1311. D1473/50/1

Derby Local Studies Library

   Derby Canal Records, D76

   Evans Papers, D162

   Strutt Letters, D125/1-50

Corporation of London Records Office, Guildhall Library

   Royal Exchange and Sun Fire Office, Insurance Registers

Sheffield Archives

   Barker Mss. D193-4

Manchester Local Studies Unit Archives

   Samuel Oldknow Papers

   Strutt Papers

Papers in private possession

   Arkwright Mss

   Chatsworth Mss (Devonshire Papers)

   Strutt Mss

2. Official Publications

(a) Parliamentary Papers

House of Lords Committee on the Health and Morals of Apprentices and others employed in Cotton and other mills etc.   1818 (90) XCVI

House of Lords: An account of the Cotton and Woollen Mills and Factories in the United Kingdom   1819 (66) III

House of Lords Committee on the State and Condition of Children employed in the Cotton Manufactories of the United Kingdom   1819 (24) CX

Royal Commission on the Employment of Children in Factories, 1st Report   1833 (450) XX

Royal Commission on the Employment of Children in Factories. Supplementary Reports   1834 (167) XIX, XX

Select Committee on the State of Children employed in the Manufactories of the United Kingdom   1816 (397) III

(b) Maps

Ordnance Survey: 25 inches to 1 mile; 1st edition (c.1888) (Derwent Valley area)

(c) Patents Library

Patent Specification No 931 Arkwright's Waterframe 1769

Patent Specification No 1111 Arkwright's Carding Engine 1775

3. Printed Primary Sources

Newspapers

The Times

The Derby Mercury

4. Printed Secondary Sources

Adam, W	The Gem of the Peak	1851
Albert, W	The Turnpike Road System in England 1663-1840	1972
Aldous, A	Britain's Industrial Heritage seeks World Status History Today, vol. 49	1999
Anderson, P H	Forgotten Railways: The East Midlands	1973
Andrews, C B (ed.)	The Torrington Diaries	1935
Architecture East Midlands	Cromford Mills Project	Sept 1980
Arkwright Society	Arkwright and the Mills at Cromford	1971
Arkwright Society	Arkwright; the man, his mills and the Industrial Revolution	1982
Ashmore, O	The Early Textile Industry in the Derwent Valley. Derbyshire Miscellany Vol.	1957
Aspin, C	The Cotton Industry	1995
Baines, E	A History of the Cotton Manufacture in Great Britain	1835
Bannister, Turpin	The First Iron Framed Buildings Architectural Review 131	1962
Barnes, T & Fairbairn, W	Lancashire and Cheshire Past and Present, Vol. II	1867
Becket, J V	The East Midlands from AD 1000	1988

Belper Historical Society	Belper: A Study of its History Based on Visual Evidence	1971
Berg, Maxine	The Age of the Manufacturers 1700-1820. Industry, Innovation and Work in Britain	1994
Billson, P	Derby and the Midland Railway	1996
Bray, William	Sketch of a Tour into Derbyshire and Yorkshire 2nd Edition	1783
British Library Science Reference Library	Rex versus Arkwright	1985
Britton, J and Brayley, E W	The Beauties of England and Wales	1802
Brunskill, R W	Illustrated Handbook of Vernacular Architecture	1987
Bryan, Ben	Matlock Manor and Town	1903
Buchanan, R A	Industrial Archaeology in Britain	1980
Bulmer & Co.	History Topography and Directory of Derbyshire	1895
Bulmer, T	North Street, Cromford Transactions of Ancient Monument Society vol. 20	1975
Burton, Anthony	Remains of a Revolution	1975
Butt, John	The Industrial Archaeology of Scotland	1967
Butterton, H E	Silk Milk: Derby's Historic Riverside Industry The Old Derby Silk Mill and its Rivals	1996 1996
Calladine, A	Lombe's Mill: An Exercise in Reconstruction Industrial Archaeological Review vol.16 No.1 Autumn	1993
Calladine, A and Fricker, J	Cheshire Textile Mills	1993
Cavendish, R	The Arkwright Society. Restoration of the 1771 Mill and Warehouse at Cromford History Today vol. 41	1991
Chaloner, W H	Sir Thomas Lombe 1685-1739 and the British Silk Industry History Today Vol. 3	1953
Chambers, J D	Industrialisation as a factor in economic growth in England	1700-1900.
	First International Conference on Economic History	1960
Chambers, J D	Review of "The Strutts and the Arkwrights" by Fitton and Wadsworth, Business History, III	1959-60
Chambers, J D	Foreword to the Arkwright Festival Prospectus	1970
Chambers, J D	The Vale of Trent 1670-1800: A Regional study of Economic Change. Economic History Review	1957
Chambers, J D	The Rural Domestic Industries during the transition to the factory system. Transactions of the first International Conference of Economic History	1961
Chambers, J D	The Workshop of the World, British Economic History from 1820- 1880	1967
Chambers, J D	Three Essays on the Population and the Economy Ed. D V Glass and D E C Eversley	1965

Chambers, J D and Barley, M W	Industrial Monuments at Milford and Belper Archaeological Review vol. 18	1961
Chapman, S D	The Beginnings of Industrial Britain	1970
Chapman, S D	The Arkwright Mills: Colquhouns Census 1788 and Archaeological Evidence Industrial Archaeological Review vol. 6 No. 1	1981
Chapman, S D	The Early Factory Masters 2nd Edition	1992
Chapman, S D	The Cotton Industry in the Industrial Revolution 2nd Edition	1987
Chapman, S D	The Textile Factory before Arkwright. A typology of Factory Development Business History Review vol. 32 No. 1	1974
Chapman, S D	Fixed Capital Formation in the British Cotton Industry 1770-1815 Economic History Review 2nd Series vol. 23 No. 2	1970
Chapman, S D	Workers' Housing in the Factory Colonies 1770-1850 Textile History vol. 7	1976
Chapman, S D	Financial restraints on the growth of firms in the Cotton Industry; 1790-1850, Economic History Review, 2nd series vol. XXXII, No. 1	1979
Chapman, S D	James Longsdon (1745-1821) farmer and fustian manufacturer. The small firm in the English Cotton Industry, Textile History, No. 3.	1970
Cooke, A J	Richard Arkwright and the Scottish Cotton Industry. Textile Industry No. 10	1979
Cookson, G	Innovation, diffusion and mechanical engineers in Britain 1780-1850. Economic History Review Vol. 47	1994
Cooper, Brian	Transformation of a Valley. The Derbyshire Derwent	1997
Cossons, Neil	The BP Book of Industrial Archaeology	1993
Cromford Canal Society	The Cromford Canal and Leawood Pump	1975
Daniels, S	Joseph Wright	1999
Dartington Amenity Research Trust	Interpreting the Derwent Valley	1979
Darwin, E	The Botanic Garden	1789-91
Davies, D P	A Historical and Descriptive View of Derbyshire	1811
Davies, J	A collection of the most important cases respecting patents, inventions and the rights of patents	1816
Davis, H D	History You Can See - Scenes of Change in Rhode Island 1790-1910 League of Rhode Island Historical Societies, Providence	1986
Die Macht der Maschine	200 Jahre Cromford-Ratingen	1985
Dutton, H I	The Patent System and Inventive Activity during the Industrial Revolution 1750-1852	1984
Edwards, M M	The Growth of British Cotton Trade 1780-1815	1967
Encyclopedia Britannica	(on Cotton Manufacture)	1824 edition
English, W	The Textile Trade	1969
Fairbairn, W	Treatise on Mills and Millwork Vol. 2	1863

Falconer, K A	The Guide to England's Industrial Heritage	1980
Falconer, K A	Fire proof Mills: The Widening Perspective Industrial Archaeological Review vol. 16	1993
Falconer, K A	Textile Mills and the Royal Commission Industrial Archaeological Review vol. 16 No. 1	1993
Farey, J	Agriculture of Derbyshire Vol. 2	1813
Felkin, W	History of the Machine Wrought Hosiery and Lace Manufactures	1867
Fielden, J	The Curse of the Factory System	1836
Fitton, R S	The Arkwrights. Spinners of Fortune	1989
Fitton, R S and Wadsworth, A P	The Strutts and the Arkwrights 1758-1830	1958
Fitzgerald, R	The Development of the Cast Iron frame in Textile Mills to 1850. Industrial Archaeology Review vol. 10	1987
Gentleman's	Magazine Library English Topography Part 3 (Derbyshire-Dorset)	1893
Giles, C and Goodall, I H	Yorkshire Textile Mills 1770-1930	1992
Glover, S	History and Gazeteer of Derbyshire vol. II	1833
Glover, S	The Peak Guide	1830
Goodwin, A	A study of Industrial Villages in Derbyshire	1977
Gordon and Malone	Texture of Industry	1994
Guest, R	A Compendious History of Cotton Manufacture	1823
Hadfield, E R C	British Canals: An Illustrated History	1979
Harris, J R	Industrial Espionage and Technology Transfer	1997
Hartle, N B	History of George Brettle and Co.	1973
Henson, G	The Civic Political and History of Framework Knitters in Europe and America	1831
Hewish, J	From Cromford to Chancery Lane. Technology and Culture vol. 28	1987
Hills, R L	Power in the Industrial Revolution	1970
Hills, R L	Hargreaves, Arkwright and Crompton. Why Three Inventors? Textile History Review No. 10	1979
Hills, R L	Richard Arkwright and Cotton Spinning	1973
Holden, R N	Stott and Sons	1998
Hume, John R	The Industrial Archaeology of New Lanark and Robert Owen, Prince of Cotton Spinners. edited John Butt	1971
Hume, John R	The Industrial Archaeology of Scotland volume I	1976
Hutton, W	History of Derby	1817
Jenkins, D T	The Cotton Industry in Yorkshire 1780-1910, Textile History No. 10	1987
Jennison, B	The Building of the Railway Park Review No. 19	1966
Jeremy, D J (editor)	Transatlantic Industrial Revolution	1981

Johnson, H R and Skempton, A W	William Strutt's Cotton Mills 1793-1850 Transactions of the Newcomen Society vol. 30	1955-57
Joyce, B	The Derwent Valley. Derbyshire Life and Countryside, Vol. 64 No. 8	1999
Kennedy, J	Observations on the Rise and Progress of the Cotton Trade in Great Britain. Memoirs of the Manchester Philosophical Society, 2nd series III	1819
King-Hele, D	Doctor of Revolution. The life and genius of Erasmus Darwin	1977
King-Hele, D	Erasmus Darwin A life of unequalled achievement	1999
Klima, A	Economy Industry and Society in Bohemia in the 17th-19th Centuries	1991
Klingender, Francis D	Art and the Industrial Revolution	1975
Langford, Paul	A Polite and Commercial People: England 1727-1783	1998
Lawrence, J S	History of Textiles	1912
Lindsay, J	An Early Industrial Community: The Evans Cotton Mill at Darley Abbey, Derbyshire 1783-1810 Business History Review vol. 34	1960
Lindstrum, D	West Yorkshire Architects and Architecture	1978
Masters, B	Georgiana	1981
Mathias, P	The First Industrial Revolution, an Economic History of Britain 1700-1914 (2nd edition)	1983
Mathias, P	The transformation of England: Essays in the Economic and Social History of England in the 18th Century	1979
Menuge, A	The Cotton Mills of the Derbyshire Derwent and its tributaries. Industrial Archaeological Review vol.16 no.1	1993
Montgomery, James	A Practical Detail of the Cotton Manufacture of the United States of America	1840
Moore, H	Picturesque Excursions from Derby to Matlock Bath	1818
Moritz, K	Travels through Several Parts of England in 1782	1926
Musson, A E	Science and Technology in the Industiral Revolution	1969
Nicholson, Benedict	Joseph Wright of Derby. Painter of Light vols. 1 and 2	1968
Nixon, Frank	Industrial Archaeology of Derbyshire	1969
O'Brien, P.K. & Quinault R	The Industrial Revolution and British Society	1993
Page, W (editor)	Victorian History of the Counties of England: Derbyshire vol. II	1907
Palmer, M R and Neaverson, P	Industrial Landscapes of the East Midlands	1992
Pawson, E	Transport and Economy: The Turnpike Roads of 18th Century Britain	1977
Peters, Don	Darley Abbey: From Monastery to Industrial Community	1974
Pevsner, N	The Buildings of England: Derbyshire 2nd edition	1978

4. Select Bibliography

Philips, Sir Richard	A Personal Tour through the United Kingdom Describing Living Objects and Contemporary Interests	1828
Pilkington, J	View of the present state of Derbyshire vol. 2	1789
Power, E G	Belper: First Cotton Mill Town, Belper Historical Society	1998
Pugh, Kate	Estate Villages Who Cares? Save Britain's Heritage	1983
Rees, Abraham	The Cyclopaedia or Universal Dictionary of Arts, Science and Literature 1819-1820 Ed. Neil Cossons	1972
Rhode Island	Department of the Environment Working Water - A Guide to the Historic Landscape of the Blackstone River Valley	1987
Richards, J M	The Functional Tradition in Early Industrial Buildings	1958
Rimer, A	Cromford and High Peak Railway	1985
Rivard, P E	Samuel Slater - Father of American Manufacturers	1974
Rodgers, B	Cloak of Charity: Studies in 18th Century Philanthropy	1949
Ross, Michael	Planning and the Heritage	1991
Rowland, K T	Eighteenth Century Inventor	1974
Schinkel, K F	The English Journey	1993
Schofield, R B	The Promotion of the Cromford Canal in 1789, a study in Canal engineering. Bulletin of John Rylands Library No. 54.	1981-82
Schopenhauer, Johanna	A Lady Travels	1988
Singer, C & others	A History of Technology Vol IV. The Industrial Revolution c.1750-c.1850	1958
Skempton, A W and Johnson, H R	William Strutt's Cotton Mills 1793-1812 Transactions of the Newcomen Society vol. 30	1955-7
Smiles, Samuel	Self-Help (on Richard Arkwright)	
Smith, D M	The Silk Industry of the East Midlands	1962
Stratton, M	Industrial Buildings Conservation and Regeneration	2000
Stratton, M R and Trinder, B	Industrial England	1997
Strutt, F	Jedediah Strutt: Memorials of old Derbyshire, edited by Cox, J C	1907
Swindon, K	The Arkwright Cotton Mills at Cromford Journal of Industrial Archaeology vol .2 No. 1	1965
Tann, Jennifer	The Development of the Factory	1970
Tann, Jennifer	Richard Arkwright and Technology Textile History vol.10 pp114-196	1973
TICCIH	The International Industrial Sites List	1994
Trinder, Barrie	The Making of the Industrial Landscape	1992
Trinder, Barrie	The Blackwell Encyclopaedia of Industrial Archaeology	1992
Unsworth, W	Portrait of the River Derwent	1971

Unwin, S and others	Samuel Oldknow and the Arkwrights	1924
Ure, A	The Philosophy of Manufactories	1861
Warner, R	A Tour through the Northern Counties of England and the Borders of Scotland	1802
White, G S	Memoir of Samuel Slater	1836
Williams, M & others	Cotton Mills in Greater Manchester	1992
Williamson, F	George Sorocold of Derby Journal of the Derbyshire Archaeological Society vol. 11	1889
Winter, John	Industrial Architecture	1970
Woodall, F D	Steam Engines and Waterwheels	1975
Wyke, T	Cotton: A Select Bibliography on Cotton in North West England	1997
Young, A	A Six Months Tour through the North of England	1770

4 (b) A Glossary of terms used in this volume

Article 4 Direction - a planning measure which brings under control minor works, normally exempt from control.

China Mill – a mill which mixed and ground the materials used in the manufacture and glazing of porcelain.

Cluster House – a group of four houses within a single block. These houses were for the skilled work people and generally included features appropriate to their occupant's status such as gardens, privies exclusive to each house and, in Belper, pigcotes.

Conservation Area - a statutory designation by a local authority, of an area of special architectural or historic interest, the character or appearance of which it is desirable to preserve or enhance.

Conservation Area Partnership (CAP) - a grant aid scheme funded by local authorities and either English Heritage or the Heritage Lottery Fund, to assist the repair and enhancement of historic buildings and their setting, in a Conservation Area.

Cottonopolis - cotton city, a Victorian sobriquet for Manchester as the world centre of the cotton industry.

Countryside Stewardship Agri-environment Scheme - a scheme which makes payments to farmers and land managers to improve the natural beauty and diversity of the countryside.

Flume - an artificial watercourse. The word is often used to describe the channels which carried water to, or away from, a mill.

Fulling Mill - a mill where cloth is shrunk and compacted by vigorous pounding using water and a fulling agent. Historically this was generally human urine.

Goit or Goyt - a man-made watercourse frequently associated with the delivery of water to a mill wheel or with its discharge from the wheelpit.

Jenny - a multiple spindle spinning machine invented by James Hargreaves in the late 1760s. These machines were hand-operated and so were ideally suited to operations within a cottage or a small workshop.

Landscape Character Assessment - a method for recording the way different components of the landscape - physical, natural and cultural - interact and are perceived.

Launder - a channel often made of wood for conveying liquids.

Leat - see Goit

Lengthman - a person employed to maintain a section of road, railway or canal.

Listed Building - a statutory term for buildings of special architectural or historic interest, which are listed in three grades, I, II* or II, depending upon their level of importance.

Local Nature Reserve - a statutory designation by a local authority of an area to be managed, in the long term, for its biodiversity value.

Mule - the spinning mule was invented by Samuel Crompton, 1753-1827, in England in the 1770s. The mule did not become widespread in commercial use until the end of the century and did not reach full maturity until 1825-1830 when the fully mechanised version was developed by Richard Roberts. The mule acquired its name because it combines the drafting rollers of Arkwright's water frame with the moving carriage of Hargreave's spinning jenny.

Nail Shop - a workshop where nails were made by hand from bar iron.

Outshut - an extension to a building under a lean-to roof.

Perron - an external flight of steps and landing giving access to the piano nobile level of a building.

Peruke - a wig. A peruke maker - a person who makes wigs.

Pigcote - a small permanent housing for pig rearing which incorporates shelter and an open area for exercise. Also known as a pigsty.

Quoin, coyn or coin - usually the dressed stones which form the external angle of a building.

Registered Parks and Gardens - historic designed landscapes entered in a register which is compiled by English Heritage to draw attention to their importance.

Scheduled Ancient Monument (SAM) - a statutory designation for an archaeological site, building, earthwork or other man-made structure which can date from pre-historic to modern times and which is scheduled for its national archaeological importance.

Site of Importance for Nature Conservation (SINC) - a non-statutory designation of a site of regional or county level importance encompassing geology and biodiversity.

Site of Special Scientific Interest (SSSI) - a statutory designation of a site of national or international geological or biodiversity importance identified by English Nature.

Sough - an underground channel used to drain water from lead mines.

Special Area of Conservation (SAC) - a statutory designation of a site of European geological or biodiversity importance which contributes to the Natura 2000 Network under Article 3(1) of the Habitats Directive.

Special Landscape Area - a non-statutory designation of the finest Derbyshire landscape, outside the Peak District National Park, to which are applied special planning policies designed to preserve and enhance its character.

Stockinger - a person, usually a man, who made stockings and other clothing using a knitting frame sometimes called a stocking frame.

Throwing - the term applied to the spinning of silk by winding, doubling and twisting.

Town Scheme - a now discontinued conservation area grant aid scheme funded by local authorities and English Heritage, which has been replaced by a Conservation Area Partnership.

Tram - a lightly spun silk yarn consisting of single threads of silk doubled and gently twisted. Tram was used by silk weavers for weft yarn.

Truck - the word literally means exchange. A truck shop was the place where workers could exchange tokens or notes guaranteeing them goods to a certain value for the goods that they needed. It was a system which was open to exploitation by the factory masters. In the early industrial communities a shortage of coins encouraged factory masters to turn to the payment of wages partly in goods and services.

UK & Local Biodiversity Action Plan - strategies which contribute to the international convention on biological diversity, signed by 150 states in 1992 at the Rio Summit meeting.

Water frame - Arkwright's frame for spinning cotton, once it had been successfully driven by water, became known as the water frame and its products as water twist.

4 (c) Illustration Acknowledgements

The Derwent Valley Mills Partnership gratefully
acknowledges the assistance it has received from all those
bodies and individuals who have made available material to
illustrate this volume.

Amber Valley Borough Council, Charles Arkwright, The
Arkwright Society, Bolton Museum, The British Library,
Christopher Charlton, The Department for Culture Media and
Sport, Derby City Council, Derby Museum and Art Gallery,
The Derbyshire Archaeological Society, The Derbyshire
Building Society, Derbyshire County Council, Derbyshire
Record Office, English Heritage: National Monuments Record
©Crown Copyright NMR, Helmshore Higher Mill Museum,
Landschaftsverband Rheinland, Masson Mill, Michael Morris,
North Mill Trust Belper, The Science Museum, St Mary's
Church Cromford, Patrick Strange, John Strutt, Glynn Waite.

Many of the illustrations acknowledged here have been
prepared for publication by the *Croft Studio of Design*.
The modern photographic images of buildings have been
produced by *Martin Jones* and of archive material by
Trevor Steed. To them the editors extend their thanks.